MART

Glendale and the Revolution in Skye

MARTYRS

Glendale and the Revolution in Skye

ROGER HUTCHINSON

BIRLINN

First published in 2015 by
Birlinn Limited
West Newington House
10 Newington Road
Edinburgh
EH9 1QS

www.birlinn.co.uk

ISBN 978 1 78027 322 8

British Library Cataloguing-in-Publication Data
A catalogue record for this book is available from the British Library

Typeset by Iolaire Typesetting, Newtonmore
Printed and bound by Grafica Veneta
(www.graficaveneta.com)

To all my friends in and from Skye.
You know who you are.

Revolution, *n.* Complete change, turning upside down, reversal of conditions.

– The Concise Oxford Dictionary

Contents

List of Illustrations

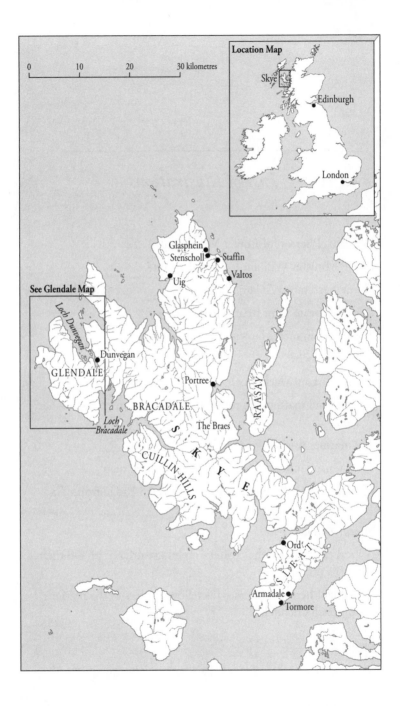

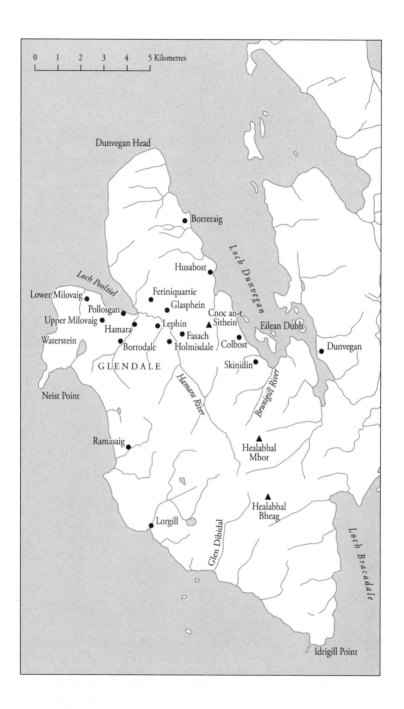

0 1 2 3 4 5 Kilometres

Dunvegan Head

Borreraig

Husabost

Loch Pooltiel

Feriniquarrie

Lower Milovaig
Pollosgan
Glasphein
Upper Milovaig
Cnoc an-t
Hamara
Lephin
Sithein
Eilean Dubh
Waterstein
Fasach
Colbost
Dunvegan
Borrodale
Holmisdale
GLENDALE
Skinidin

Loch Dunvegan

Neist Point

Hamara River

Brunigill River

Ramasaig

Healabhal
Mhor

Healabhal
Bheag

Lorgill

Loch Bracadale

Glen Dibidal

Idrigill Point

Preface

Scattered around a shoreline on the most westerly peninsula in the island of Skye, Lower Milovaig is as isolated a village as still exists in the populated Highlands. A seagull flies more quickly from Lower Milovaig to the Outer Hebridean island of North Uist than to its own Inner Hebridean island capital of Portree. Lower Milovaig is at the end of the road.

It is of course a transcendently lovely part of the most beautiful archipelago in Europe. Lower Milovaig is framed by the open Minch, the round hills of the Outer Isles, and in the immediate foreground by its own inshore waters of Loch Pooltiel and the high, riven cliffs of the Husabost peninsula. The hillside behind the township is scarred by the remnants of lazybeds and peat-cuttings. The ground which slopes from the houses down to the sea is still divided into long, rectangular crofts. Those are the vestiges of a lifestyle which, until recently, was commonplace in Skye, and which men and women once held to be so valuable that they would fight for its preservation.

There has not recently been much fighting in Lower Milovaig. Twenty-first-century visitors to the place must send their imaginations on almost impossible flights to conjure moving pictures of men with long hair and beards, wearing coarse, untailored homespun trousers and jackets, carrying cudgels, shouting information and encouragement at each other in Gaelic, running out of Lower Milovaig while alarms were blown on horns from neighbouring heights; of those men, followed by their wives and with their children sprinting at their flanks, racing down the track to join battle with policemen at the Hamara bridge in central Glendale. It is difficult to picture armed marines slipping ashore here in the dead of night and scurrying through the crofts to make arrests. But those scenes, and many others, unfolded within the lifetime of a Lower Milovaig adult's grandmother.

As a result there are two milestones in the history of the Highlands and Islands of Scotland which require, not diminution, but slight readjustment.

The first is that the Battle of the Braes in Skye in 1882 was the key event in the land war of the late 19th century. The second is that the Stornoway Trust, which was established in Lewis in 1923 largely as a result of the continuing Hebridean land struggle, was the first community-owned estate in a region which is, in the 21st century, bulging with community-owned estates.

Those events and that institution were and remain monumental. The courageous men and women who fought for the return of common grazings in Braes, and the people who founded and continue to run the democratic land trust in and around Stornoway, have earned an indelible place in history.

They were not, however, alone. As several modest voices from the north-west of Skye have mentioned over the decades, it was the revolution (I use the word carefully) on the Glendale estate in the 1880s which forced the hand of the Government and led directly both to the Napier Commission of inquiry into crofters' conditions in 1883 and the epochal Crofters' Act of 1886. Glendale also became, in 1905, 18 years before Lord Leverhulme gifted the most valuable portion of his Lewis property to its people, the first community-owned estate in the Highlands.

It is not the case that Glendale has been ignored by historians. The central figure in the Glendale revolt, John MacPherson, has been celebrated for over a century as the Glendale Martyr and occasionally as the Skye Martyr. In more recent times the handle has been made plural and several of John MacPherson's friends and neighbours have joined him, in death, as a body of brothers-in-arms widely known as the Glendale Martyrs.

It is, however, the case that the pivotal significance of Glendale, in provoking William Gladstone's administration to instigate a thorough inquiry and then to pass vital legislation, and in trailblazing the crofters' right and ability to own and to manage their land, has too rarely been acknowledged and that its full story has not been told.

Its full story may not, of course, ever be told. It is several decades since even the youngest players in that fierce drama slipped off this mortal coil. The narrative of what happened in Glendale throughout the 19th century can now be pieced together only from second- and third-generation recollections, from letters in archives, from state papers, from court and other legal documents, from testimony to official inquiries and from the valuable but fallible reports of contemporary journalists and authors.

Whatever the limitations of those sources, they push ajar the door to an irresistible tale. Not only did the late-Victorian people of Glendale change the course of history – of their own history and that of hundreds of thousands of others – they did so in a remarkable manner. For a significant period of time those men with beards and cudgels, and their wives, and their teen-aged children, issued a unilateral declaration of independence from the rest of the United Kingdom.

They denied the legitimate power of their landowners to collect rent and restrict their grazings. They denied the right of the authorities to station policemen in their midst. They contemptuously dismissed edicts of the courts in Portree, Inverness and Edinburgh. They drove representatives of the landowner and of the state out of their district with physical might. For a few years the 2,000 people of Glendale were the Highland equivalent of the Paris Commune: ordering their own affairs; enforcing their own laws; keeping their own peace; brooking no interference.

Try to do all that in the 21st century and see where it gets you. As Professor James Hunter said when we first discussed this book, 'The remarkable thing was the Gladstone Government's response: they sent a senior civil servant to negotiate with the Glendale crofters as if, for all the world, they were an independent power. Today you'd just get several months in jail.' In fact, as Professor Hunter knows, the Gladstone Government had no serious alternative to treating the people of Glendale as an independent power. They had already established themselves as one. The Government could either negotiate with them or use military power against them. Ultimately, it would do both.

There are many people in Scotland – you can encounter them without trying very hard – who consider Scottish Gaels to be a defeated people, who believe that Highlanders and Hebrideans meekly surrendered the land war of the 19th century and effectively dumped themselves and their culture into the bin-bag of history. If this story of what happened in Glendale and elsewhere in Skye in the course of the 1880s helps just one of those Lowlanders to reconsider his or her views, it will have served. It is as true a story as I can tell, and it is one of conviction, courage and of ultimate victory.

Over the decades I have taken lessons in the history of Skye from too many people to remember, let alone credit here. This book owes a special debt to six of them. Ian Blackford of Lower Milovaig offered selfless assistance and encouragement while successfully campaigning to become my Member of Parliament, and we both know that the two were not connected. Morna MacLaren was, as ever, the writer's perfect librarian: direct, knowledgeable, precise and great company. It is admirable in more ways than one that first-source archival material concerning Skye has been moved from Inverness to Portree, where it is now in the excellent hands of Anne MacLeod in the Skye and

Lochalsh Archive Centre. Bob O'Hara once again negotiated on my behalf the dusty maze of the National Archives at Kew.

Two old friends proved to be particularly useful. In his retirement from the chair of history at the University of the Highlands and Islands, James Hunter felt free to lend his formidable advisory powers to me. UHI's loss was my gain. Jim's enthusiasm and ability subtly to point a student in the right direction were as valuable as his fathomless knowledge.

I have known Allan Campbell for even longer than I have known Jim Hunter. I was always aware that Allan comes from Colbost. I always knew that he had an intimate acquaintanceship with the astonishing history of Glendale. I could never have guessed that he would be so generous, energetic and unstinting with his time and intellect. Moran taing, Ailean.

Many thanks also to my editor Helen Bleck, to Hugh Andrew and everybody else at that fine independent publishing house, Birlinn, and to my agent Stan.

Roger Hutchinson,
Raasay, 2015

ONE

A Problem in the Provinces

THE LORD PRESIDENT of the Court of Session had a problem in the provinces.

John Inglis, Lord Glencorse, was a 72–year-old son of the manse. He had been born in Edinburgh in 1810, educated at the universities of Glasgow and Oxford, and had risen to become Solicitor General for Scotland at the age of 42 years. His distinguished legal career elevated him to the title of Lord Glencorse and then, in 1867, to the head of the judiciary in Scotland.

In the morning of 11 January 1883, John Inglis, Lord Glencorse, Fellow of the Royal Society of Edinburgh and the Lord President of the Court of Session, was told by a landowner's lawyer that five crofters 250 miles away in the island of Skye had broken earlier interdicts against trespass. They had also, it was alleged, recently assaulted a shepherd. It was therefore necessary to summon them to appear before the bar in Edinburgh.

The petition and complaint were presented to Lord Glencorse's Court of Session by Thomas Graham Murray of the distinguished Edinburgh solicitors Tods Murray & Jamieson. Thomas Murray represented the trustees of the property of the late owner of the estate of Glendale in Skye, Sir John Macpherson MacLeod, Knight Commander of the Order of the Star of India, who had died two years earlier.

On that Thursday morning in January 1883, the pantheon

of Scottish high society which was represented by Thomas Graham Murray, Lord Glencorse and two other law lords found itself debating how best to summon five crofters from Skye to Edinburgh.

'I have to ask your lordships,' said Murray. 'to pronounce an order ordaining the respondents to appear at the bar. In the special circumstances of this case I shall ask your lordships to allow us to send the order by registered letter.'

'What is the order you ask for?' said Glencorse.

'The order I ask for is to ordain the respondents to appear at the bar,' said Murray.

'How many respondents are there?' asked Glencorse's colleague at the bar, Lord David Mure.

'There are five of them,' said Thomas Murray.

The Lord President of the Court of Session said that he could not understand the 'special circumstances' which had led Thomas Murray to suggest sending the court order to Skye by registered letter. Lord Glencorse was standing by the letter of the law, but he was also being sophistical. By January 1883 virtually every literate person in Scotland knew of the 'special circumstances' which obtained in Skye. 'Have you any precedent for that mode of sending an order, Mr Murray?' asked Lord Glencorse.

'No, my lord,' said Murray, 'there is no authority. I think the matter is entirely in your lordships' hands. The matter is not regulated by any express enactment. The Act of Sederunt that deals with it is 28, which simply says that the procedure shall be, so far as possible, the same as the procedure in a petition and complaint against the freeholders.

'Your lordships see that this is really simply intimating an order of Court,' said Murray, attempting a different tack, 'and one great reason for this, without directing your attention to any other special circumstances, is the very large expense that is incurred by service in such a remote part. The service in this case practically costs £40. Now, there have already been three services. There was first the original service of interdict; and then there was the service of interim interdict; and then, lastly, there was the service of the petition and complaint.'

Despite the expense of delivering interdicts by hand, despite the 'special circumstances' in Skye, their Lordships were deeply reluctant to serve Court of Session orders through the mail.

'Is there any messenger-at-arms?' asked Lord Glencorse.

'There is nobody nearer than Glasgow or Inverness,' said Thomas Murray.

'What do you say the expense was?' asked Lord Mure.

'Forty pounds on each occasion. Thirty pounds of fee, and £10 of expenses,' said Murray.

'Is there a Sheriff Court officer in Skye?' asked Lord Glencorse.

'There is a sheriff-substitute at Skye if there is not a sheriff officer,' Lord Mure informed his superior.

At that, the Lord President told Thomas Murray that their lordships would convene in camera and deliver a decision on how to serve their court orders later in the day. That afternoon they reassembled and announced that they 'did not see their way to grant the request to serve the order by registered letter'. Tods Murray & Jamieson would just have to serve it in the ordinary way.

The court would make an order for the respondents to appear personally at the bar, but Lord Glencorse thought that 'probably they had better make it so many days after service'. He supposed it was a matter of no consequence whether they authorised it to be done by a sheriff officer rather than a messenger-at-arms.

Defeated in his well-founded efforts to entrust the summonses to the Royal Mail rather than to the person of a sheriff officer, Mr Murray said that it would be better if he had the option of employing a messenger-at-arms. He would not like to be tied down to employing a sheriff officer. He did not say so in the Court of Session, but Murray had very good reasons for that strategy.

In the afternoon of 11 January 1883, therefore, the Court of

Session in Edinburgh, 'in respect of no answer and no appearance for the respondents', made an order for the five accused to appear personally at the bar on 1 February, provided the order was served on them ten days before that date. The court authorised either a sheriff officer or messenger-at-arms to serve the order on John MacPherson, Malcolm Matheson, Donald MacLeod, Donald Ferguson and John Morrison of Glendale in Skye. They were aged between 22 and 59 years, and all five of them lived in the small adjoining hamlets of Upper and Lower Milovaig.

Later that same day a 55—year-old messenger-at-arms who was living in the Mount Florida district of Glasgow was instructed by Tods Murray & Jamieson to proceed to Skye to pursue an order of the Court of Session. Of all the messengers-at-arms in the Scottish Lowlands, Donald MacTavish was chosen for the task for two important reasons. He had been born and raised in the rural Inverness-shire township of Dores and was a native speaker of Gaelic, which was in 1883 the default or only language of the people of Glendale. He had also recently visited Skye on similar business.

MacTavish's Highland background and experience of Skye would have given him an even better understanding than Thomas Murray, Lord Glencorse and Lord Mure of the potential difficulties of his commission. He might have been aware that he was approaching a lions' den. But even he cannot have anticipated the chaos, fury and violence which were to follow, let alone the consequences for the future of the north of Scotland.

Donald MacTavish left on the evening train from Glasgow on the following Monday, 15 January, and arrived in north-west Skye two days later. The remit of a messenger-at-arms of the Scottish Court of Session in 1883 was virtually identical to that of a sheriff officer. Both were responsible for serving documents and enforcing court orders.

The difference was that a sheriff officer was limited to his Sheriff Court district. In the case of Glendale that district was the island of Skye, whose Sheriff Court, of which Lords Glencorse and Mure were happily ignorant, was in the main township of Portree. Under normal circumstances a Skye-based sheriff officer attached to Portree Sheriff Court would have been sent into Glendale with court orders. As Thomas Murray had been so anxious to point out, normal circumstances did not, however, pertain in Skye early in 1883.

A messenger-at-arms was licensed to operate nationally. Having been frustrated by the law lords in their attempt to have the summonses sent by mail, Thomas Murray of Tods Murray & Jamieson and their employers, the trustees of the Glendale estate, had excellent motives for deploying a messenger-at-arms from faraway Glasgow rather than a local sheriff officer. Donald MacTavish was well aware of the source of those motives.

Six mornings after that fateful hearing before Lord Glencorse in the Scottish Court of Appeal, at midday on Wednesday, 17 January 1883, the messenger-at-arms Donald MacTavish left his hotel in the township of Dunvegan in north-western Skye for the rural crofting lands of Glendale. He had attached to his chest his distinctive silver blazon, without which he could not legally assert his authority, and was carrying the rod of office known as a wand of peace. MacTavish was also accompanied by a nervous sheriff officer from Roag near Dunvegan named Angus MacLeod, who had been persuaded to bear witness. MacLeod was known locally as Aonghas Dubh, or Black Angus.

Looking west from Dunvegan, two gargantuan flat-topped mountains stand sentinel over the broad peninsula of Glendale. Those mesas, the 1539–foot high Healabhal Mhor and its slightly taller but slimmer twin, the 1600–foot Healabhal Bheag, are volcanic plugs which, like much of the rest of the hillscape of the north-west Highlands and Islands of Scotland, were thrown up by an eruption 60 million years ago. In 1883 they were already better known as MacLeod's Tables. They are not hysterical, careless mountains like the Cuillins to their south, or gently beckoning like the hills of Uist across the water to the west. They are brooding and peculiar and somehow out of place, like transplants from Monument Valley. They could in certain lights be seen as ominous.

Donald MacTavish and Angus MacLeod passed the lower slopes of Healabhal Mhor and strode through the scattered thatched crofthouses at Skinidin shortly after noon. They walked northwards, with the hills to their left and the sea immediately to their right. They were still almost six miles from Milovaig, where most of the writs were to be served.

Just beyond Skinidin, in the township of Colbost, Donald MacTavish lost the company of Sheriff Officer Angus MacLeod. The two men called at Colbost House, the large dwelling of the MacRaild family. Its patriarch, the 80–year-old Norman MacRaild, was a former factor of the MacPherson estates. His son, 48–year-old James MacRaild, was currently the ground officer, or local representative of the trustees of the MacPherson estate in Glendale. MacTavish and MacLeod were told that James MacRaild had gone on ahead and was waiting for the messenger-at-arms three miles further along the road, at the bridge over the River Hamara in central Glendale. They were also told that the Sheriff Officer Black Angus MacLeod 'was threatened by the tenants'. Angus MacLeod prudently decided to wait in the MacRaild property at Colbost House for Donald MacTavish to return. Over in Glendale, James MacRaild could bear witness to MacTavish's writs.

MacTavish strode on alone, away from Loch Dunvegan, up and over Cnoc an t-Sìthein, or Colbost Hill, a short but shadowy pass across a watershed. He saw nobody, but from the hilltops around him the messenger-at-arms heard horns being blown in warning, and he heard their blasts repeated in echoes far away to the west and north. As he crossed the summit of Cnoc an t-Sìthein he lost sight of the comforting bulk of the rest of the island of Skye. Instead, hundreds of thatched houses issuing peat smoke lay below him in half-a-dozen busy villages scattered around the head of a sea loch, on the broad floor and lower slopes of an isolated glen. He would not have seen his ultimate destination of Upper and Lower Milovaig. They were sheltered by the low hills and meandering shoreline another couple of miles beyond the River Hamara.

But he will have seen, for the first time since entering northwest Skye, a large crowd of people at the other side of the bridge over the River Hamara.

The single policeman based in Glendale, Constable Alexander MacVicar, was watching from below and had reason to fear the worst. That morning Constable MacVicar had left his station and set off on his rounds, 'and on my reaching the Post Office there were about eighty of the Milivaig tenants there armed with sticks.

'I called in the Post Office and the most of them followed and the rest were about the door. I found that they were waiting for Mr MacTavish.

'The people were assembling to the Post Office from all directions for this purpose. I remained there until MacTavish and the Ground Officer came around 1 p.m. The crowd met them at the Glendale Bridge and immediately turned them.' One man, said Constable MacVicar, 'ran from the crowd and bawled out to come and turn me, but all the rest told him to be quiet'.

Messenger-at-arms Donald MacTavish did, as had been prearranged, meet Ground Officer James MacRaild at the eastern approach to the bridge over the River Hamara. They got no further.

'I met at the Fasach side of the bridge crossing the Glendale [Hamara] River,' MacTavish later told the police, 'a crowd of crofters and others numbering from sixty to seventy who had been waiting at the Glendale Post Office, on seeing us coming down the Brae at Fasach came along to the Bridge to meet us, all this time the horn was blowing which was the signal for assembling the crofters from all parts of the Glen.

'On meeting the crowd I had my blazon displayed on my breast and held my wand of peace in my hand, one of the crowd took hold of me and placed a short stick to my breast and with the assistance of other two or three gave me a push which shoved me back some four or five yards, saying, "turn back now, you won't be allowed to go further towards Milivaig".

'I said "I am a messenger-at-arms from the Court of Session proceeding to serve the orders of the Court of Session upon some crofters at Milivaig". I produced and began to read a certified copy of said orders to the crowd and all this time was being pushed along the road back to Dunvegan, assaulted with sticks, pelted with stones, clods, mud and dung off the road, and very frequently tripped, causing me to fall on my face on the road, [and I] was in this manner pushed before the crowd towards Fasach, Colbost and Skinidin townships, a distance of fully four miles . . .'

Back on the westward side of the bridge, the helpless Constable Alexander MacVicar saw the crofters 'pushing and shoving MacTavish and throwing pail fulls of water and gutters about his head. They had also an old bag full of gutters and they were striking them with this.' 'Gutters' was mud and household waste, possibly leavened with sewage. Donald MacTavish did not mention this particular humiliation. The Glendale postmaster, a 55-year-old Crimean War veteran named Peter MacKinnon from Lephin in the centre of the glen, who was present and was entirely sympathetic with his neighbours, shortly afterwards denied 'that the people deforced MacTavish, till MacTavish lifted a stick; and then a half-witted lad threw a pail of water about his ears'. The stick lifted by MacTavish was presumably his wand of peace.

Whatever the substance in the pail, the messenger-at-arms noted that the crowd of angry crofters quickly grew to 'two hundred men and boys'. Two years later, in June 1885, the *Oban Times* newspaper published a victory chant of the incident by a Glendale bard who called himself 'A' Chreag Mhor' ('The Great Rock') and who was possibly among the 200 men and boys. At first sight of the Ground Officer James MacRaild, related A' Chreag Mhor, there was a cry of 'Glacadh beo e, Am poll-mona gun cuir sinn e.' ('Let him be caught alive so that we can put him in a peat bog.') 'Ach ghabh iad doigh a b' fhearr . . .' he continued, 'But they employed a better method: he was very nearly drowned . . .'

Those 200 drove Donald MacTavish and the Ground Officer James MacRaild through Fasach, over the pass again and back through Colbost and Skinidin. 'When meeting any person on the road going the contrary way,' said MacTavish, 'the crowd to show their supposed bravery would renew their attacks of pushing us at our backs with sticks, kicking, tripping, stones and dirt throwing, shouting and hurraying, and this they always did when passing the crofters' houses along the townships of Fasach, Colbost and Skinidin.'

Immediately to the south of Skinidin the crowd forced Donald MacTavish and James MacRaild over the Brunigill burn. That small tributary of Loch Dunvegan marked the boundary between the estate of the late Sir John MacPherson MacLeod at Glendale and the residual properties of MacLeod of MacLeod. A hundred years later a son of Milovaig who had not been born at the time said that he had been told that MacTavish and MacRaild were 'vomiting blood' by the time they crossed the bridge over the Brunigill. Another descendant of the crofters was told that James MacRaild had begged to be allowed to return home to Colbost House, but his assailants would have none of it. They were determined to drive the 'law-enforcers' across the estate boundary.

The crofters themselves did then return to Colbost, went to the MacRaild dwelling at Colbost House 'and took Angus MacLeod the sheriff officer at Roag out of the house and put him on the road.' 'Bha Aonghas Dubh a Roag . . .' recalled A' Chreag Mhor, 'Black Angus from Roag was seeking mercy from Norman [MacRaild] and when the pursuers came, they were all pacified . . . Norman said, shouting aloud . . . "One after the other of them was employed by myself, but when they became rebels, they would not listen to me any longer."'

MacTavish, MacRaild and MacLeod were collected at the
east side of the Brunigill bridge in a carriage which had been
despatched by the proprietrix of the Dunvegan Hotel. Once he
was safely back inside the hotel, Donald MacTavish felt 'pain
on the right leg and on the right side of my body caused by
being struck by the crofters' sticks and the stones with which
they were assaulting me. James MacRaild who was also with me
was also assaulted in the same way as I was tho' not to such an
extent.' Angus MacLeod was apparently unharmed.

'MacThabhais an t-sumanaidh . . .' wrote A' Chreag Mhor,
'MacTavish of the summonsing will never again serve us with a
notice; he almost met his death when we left him in Brunigill.
It was the hostess in the Dunvegan change-house who provided
you with a means of transport, King above, I was amazed that it
wasn't smashed to dust . . . You earned your pay dearly . . . you
would have been better gathering shellfish than be engaged in
such dangerous officership.'

Back in Glendale, Constable MacVicar, a 29–year-old bach-
elor from North Uist in the Outer Hebrides who had lodged
with a Glendale family, diplomatically 'could not recognise
[any of the offending crofters] at this distance'. With the help
of James MacRaild, Messenger-at-Arms Donald MacTavish
would later list by name many of the crowd of youths and
men, several of whom were from Milovaig and two of whom
– Malcolm Matheson and John Morrison – were on his list of
summonses.

'I identified two of the Milivaig crofters, viz Archibald
Gillies in the front rank of the crowd then six or seven deep,'
said MacTavish, 'and Malcolm MacLeod at the end of the
crowd[.] Besides these two there were in the crowd who took
a leading position in opposing me and assaulting myself and
my witness [James MacRaild] Thomas MacLean son of Donald
MacLean, Milivaig, Malcolm Mathieson, Malcolm Morrison,
Alexander McLean, Roderick MacLeod, Donald MacKinnon
son of John MacKinnon, John Morrison, Allan McKinnon all

from Milivaig, and Donald Cameron from Fasach who joined the crowd at Fasach . . .'

One extremely significant name was absent from MacTavish's roll.

As darkness fell in Glendale, young Constable Alexander MacVicar felt very alone. While he had been in the Glendale post office earlier that day, he reported to his chief constable in Inverness, 'one of them . . . was squaring with his stick to my face and said that he would take my life, but I took this as being in fun'.

'The whole of the Milivaig tenants were watching last night,' wrote Constable MacVicar at his desk in the long evening of 17 January, 1883, 'and some of them were a little the worse for drink.

'They are also watching tonight. I found them today civil, but threatening by hinting at the affair . . . They were cursing and swearing supposing 600 policemen would come that they would loose [sic] their lives before they would get in . . . They told me that I would do myself here and that they would not allow anymore to come. It is questionable whether I can get to meet the other part of my district.'

That was why Thomas Murray of Tods Murray & Jamieson had wanted to put the summonses in the post. An ordinarily placid and law-abiding part of the Scottish Highlands had become a no-go zone.

TWO

The Distant Wings of a Lonely Island

I F THE ISLAND OF SKYE is, as the poet Sorley Maclean
suggested, the great dead bird of Scotland afloat in the western
ocean, it is a deceased avian with four or five wings. Skye is
composed of sizeable peninsulas of dramatically different shapes
and topography, which radiate outwards from the central core
of the Cuillin mountain range.

Before and for many years after a modern road network was
laid across the island, those peninsulas contained discrete, effectively insular communities, largely disconnected one from the
other. A native of Sleat in the south and a native of Trotternish
in the north would each regard themselves as Sgiathanaich, or
Skye people, and they would certainly know of one another's
existence, but most of them would never in their lives set foot in
the other's townships – if, indeed, they ever left their own.

One of those misshapen floating wings is the 100 square
miles of land which is loosely known as Glendale, whose
eastern borders are Loch Dunvegan and Loch Bracadale and
the isthmus between them. Glendale is the larger part of the old
parish of Duirinish, which also includes the township and castle
of Dunvegan. Across the tapering head of Loch Dunvegan the
townships of Skinidin and Colbost, which face the old castle
and its surrounding settlements over a mile of water broken by
several stepping-stone islets, are the most easterly villages of the
main district of Glendale.

Skinidin and Colbost became part of the 19th-century Glendale estate. But historically and socially they are either the first approaches to Glendale or the last outposts of north-western Skye before Colbost Hill is crossed and the townships of Fasach and Glasphein stand as gateposts to a thoroughly insular community within a larger island. Before the 1840s Glendale itself was no more than 'one valley . . . about two miles in length, which stretches from the head of Loch Poltiel [sic] in a southerly direction, until it reaches near the base of the Smaller Helvel. Its breadth is from half a mile to three quarters of a mile; its sides sloping gradually, and covered with very rich pasture. It is divided by a considerable stream, here called the Amhainn Mhor, the Large River [later the River Hamara]; a title which, however, it scarcely deserves to enjoy.'

As the crow flies, central and western Glendale are nearer, over the strip of salt water which was known in the 19th century as Uist Sound, to Benbecula and North Uist in the Outer Hebrides than to Portree, the capital of Skye. During the millennia when travel by sea was easier than travel by land, and when fishing was a primary occupation, Glendale's link to the Outer Hebrides was even more marked.

The district of Glendale grew steadily until it reached from Dunvegan Head in the north to Idrigill Point in the south, and westward to Neist Point and Waterstein. It contains mountains and glens, a large river, harbours and inlets, a hundred burns, steep cliffs and high waterfalls. It is likely to have been popu-lated as early as any other part of Skye, which is to say in the 7th millennium BC, shortly after the retreat of the last Ice Age.

The modern history of Glendale began in the Middle Ages. Dunvegan Castle, which became the ancestral seat of the heads of Clan Leod, the Macleods of MacLeod, was first raised as a Norse fortress when the island of Skye was part of the Kingdom of Norway. The MacLeods, a Norse tribe by origin, assumed control of most of Skye, including Glendale, in the 13th century AD. The MacLeod chiefs would not relinquish Glendale until the 19th century, and still held some of their Hebridean territory in the 21st century, 750 years after Norway had ceded Skye to the Kingdom of Scotland in 1266.

In 1703 Martin Martin, a native of the north of Skye who transplanted himself to London society, anticipated Sorley Maclean by asserting that 'Skie (in the antient language Skianach, i.e. wing'd) is so called because the two opposite Northern Promonteries (Vaterness lying North-west, and Trotterness North-east) resemble two wings.' Martin had probably never crossed the pass into lonely Glendale, which he referred to not once in the Skye chapter of his *Description of the Western Islands of Scotland*. His omission is illuminative. There was in the 17th and 18th centuries no particular reason for an educated young gentleman of Skye to cross Loch Dunvegan or the pass over Colbost Hill, and there were plenty of comfortable reasons for him to remain on the Dunvegan side of the loch. Even in 1841, when the provision of turnpike roads had improved greatly in the remainder of Skye and in Duirinish 'there are lines of excellent road traversing it in various directions, and every stream that crosses these lines is spanned by a bridge. The district of Glendale is the only part that is yet left in its original inaccessible state.'

It had not always been so neglected. The track north of Colbost which led to Dunvegan Head passed through the township of Borreraig. In earlier centuries the MacCrimmons of Borreraig had been hereditary pipers to the chiefs of Clan MacLeod, for which they were rewarded with decent tacks of land, and had once opened a nationally renowned piping college in their farmsteadings at Borreraig. Once upon a time the MacCrimmons 'were well educated, intermarried with highly respectable families, and were universally regarded as vastly superior to the common class of the country people'.

By the end of the 18th century their days of glory were gone. In about 1770 MacLeod of MacLeod removed from the later MacCrimmons their lieu of Borreraig farm and the family was left to fend for itself. Some emigrated, some joined the army, others became indistinguishable from their neighbours. By the late 19th century there were still two MacCrimmon families in Glendale, but their male heads of household were occupied as a tailor and a crofter. In 1883 a 48–year-old crofter and fisherman from Borreraig named Alexander MacKenzie knew about but could not personally recall any of the fabled piping MacCrimmons. There were no pipers in Glendale, he said. There was yet a descendant of the MacCrimmons living in Borreraig, but 'He is just as ourselves, running north and south for subsistence for our families.' At least some of the rest were in Canada. The archaeologist Dr Anne MacSween, whose mother was born and raised in Glendale, would write of the occasion in 1830 when the ten families of Lorgill in south Glendale were given 24 hours to join the MV *Midlothian* in Loch Snizort and be transported to Nova Scotia. One of the families removed were MacCrimmons. It is said that once in Canada the head of that family composed a well-known pipe tune titled 'The Lorgill Crofters' Farewell to Skye'.

When the First Statistical Account of Scotland was compiled in the early 1790s, the task of describing Duirinish in Skye fell to a local Church of Scotland minister, the Reverend Mr William Bethune. Reverend Bethune dated his report October 1790, and reported that the number of souls in his parish had risen from 2,568 40 years earlier to a current 3,000. The increase was despite a number of large ships having transported hundreds of emigrants from Lochs Bracadale and Dunvegan to America. 'The old people affirm,' he wrote, 'that they remember land which lay waste in several districts, not only of this parish, but in several parts of the island, for want of inhabitants to occupy them.'

William Bethune described a relatively healthy and active late-18th-century community. There was in 1790 'a more judicious and rational treatment of children and women in childbirth, than was formerly observed . . .' Above all, smallpox,

that perennial mass-murderer of humans, had been held at bay
in Skye since around 1760 by early techniques of immunisation
through a mild dose of the infection. The result was a relatively
healthy and long-lived population. 'There are at present two
men, one of them 88, the other 95, and two women, one of
them 93, and the other 97 years . . . Marriages here produce, in
general, from 5 to 12 children, and upwards. The cottages are
full of inhabitants,' reported Reverend Bethune.

'In every district of the parish, there are some weavers, male
and female, a few tailors, a blacksmith in every barony, some
boat-builders and house-carpenters.' Every married labourer
'has a small portion of land, he raises a little flax, and has a few
sheep'. The flax for linen and the sheeps' wool were essential
'so that his wife furnishes him with his whole wearing apparel'.
They grew oats, potatoes and barley and there was still plenty
of fish in the surrounding sea. 'The people go a-fishing for their
own use, or when they see an appearance of herrings. There are
very few bred seamen, but all are expert rowers, good hardy
watermen, and skilled in making a boat with sails.' Over the
next few decades Glendale would become celebrated for 'one
culinary vegetable, i.e the cabbage, which thrives better in this
parish, I believe, than anywhere else in Scotland.

'The Glendale Cabbage is known and sought after not only
throughout all Skye, but likewise in many places on the mainland; and its immense size, combined with its delicacy of flavour,
entitles it to the pre-eminence which it has attained. The seed
is said to have been obtained from a foreign vessel which was
wrecked at the foot of Glendale many years ago.'

The common people, concluded their minister, 'are blessed
with excellent parts; a liberal share of strong natural sense, and
great acuteness of understanding. They are peaceable and gentle
in their dispositions, and are very industrious when they work
for themselves; but when they work for hire or wages, they are
inclined to be lazy and indifferent; they are rather too fond of
changes and emigrations; and though they are brave and very

loyal, they are averse to the naval and military services, and are extremely disgusted with the idea of being pressed.'

The Duirinish section of the Second Statistical Account of Scotland was written 50 years after the first, in February 1841 by a young minister who had been despatched to Skye from his birthplace in Argyllshire. He may not have realised it, but Reverend Archibald Clerk reported from the district at an historical watershed.

Its population had doubled since 1750. 'The number of the inhabitants of the parish was given in 1811 at 3,227;' wrote Reverend Clerk, 'in 1821, at 4,174; in 1831, at 4,765; and now it is closely bordering on 5,000.' Duirinish, and Glendale, reflected the growth of the entire island of Skye, and indeed the whole of the rest of the north-west Highlands and Islands. In 1755 Skye was estimated to contain 11,252 people. In 1841 the National Census counted 23,082 residents on the island: its highest population level in previous or later history.

Archibald Clerk attributed the increase to both natural and sociological reasons. 'We should remember,' he wrote, 'both that population has, in all circumstances, a strong natural tendency to multiply itself, and that among an uneducated people this tendency always increases in the direct ratio of their poverty . . .

'In the olden time, the number of a chief's followers constituted his wealth, his power, and his safeguard. He then, for the most obvious reasons, gave the produce of his lands to the support of his retainers, and thus the country was capable of supporting a larger number than it is now, when so much of its produce is given as rent; and if scarcity were felt in these lawless days, a few forays or *creaghs* [a *creach* is a raid for plunder] from some other district soon supplied it.

'After the abolition of the clan system, and when rents, which were at first very light, came to be exacted, the wars in which Britain was constantly engaged for such a series of years, afforded an outlet, to a considerable extent, to the superabundant population; and many of those who did not avail themselves of this outlet emigrated to the North American colonies; thus showing much more enterprise than is manifested by their descendants.'

There was another reason. Fifty years earlier Reverend William Bethune had written from Duirinish that, 'Every species of sea-weed is reckoned most excellent manure, though it is thought to burn and waste the soil, when it is not mixed with earth, and it is reckoned more profitable to convert it into kelp, than into manure. There are some kelp-shores, and the parish makes a hundred tons annually.'

Bethune had noted the beginning of the brief west Highland kelp boom. Kelp is the large-leaved brown sea-weed which lavishly coats the shores of that district. Gathered, dried and burned, it produces soda ash, or sodium carbonate. This compound has a number of industrial uses, including the manufacture of gunpowder. As the long war between other powers and Republican and then Napoleonic France began after the French Revolution in 1789, and as the domestic industrial revolution accelerated in the south of Britain, there was unprecendented demand for home-produced sodium carbonate and therefore for Highland kelp ash.

That demand was gratefully exploited by such landowners as MacLeod of MacLeod who had been at a loss to resume their former social standing. They paid their tenants small amounts of money to harvest and burn the kelp, and then they sold it on the southern markets at substantial profits. To quote Professor James Hunter, talking in 2011: 'At the height of the boom, kelp was fetching as much as £20 a ton – more than £1,000 at today's prices. Crofters, for their part, were getting a pound or two a ton at best – with much of this being returned to crofting landlords in the shape of rent.' The landowners grew rich, improved their properties and sent their sons to Eton and Harrow. Their tenants found themselves for the first time with a tiny but dependable source of cash to spend on providing for their families.

For a few decades it seemed as though there might be a place for the Highlands in industrial Britain. As Reverend Archibald

Clerk wrote in the early 1840s, 'the manufacture of sea-ware into kelp afforded abundant employment to all the islanders who were not engaged in the tillage of the soil, and amply rewarded their labour, so as to enable them to purchase such necessaries and comforts of life as they needed.

'During these times, then, the pressure of the population on the means of subsistence was but slightly and seldom felt, and consequently there was little cause to check its growth.'

The kelp boom lasted for less than three decades. By 1815 Britain was at peace. What was more, foreign sources of mined sodium carbonate proved to be much cheaper, infinitely more plentiful and easy to import over seas which were dominated by the Royal Navy and no longer threatened by hostile warships. Within a few years, wrote Reverend Clerk, 'matters are completely changed. There is no recruiting for war. The kelp trade is completely at an end. The people do not emigrate. There are no public works where they may find employment. They raise but a very inadequate quantity of food, and they are, as the natural result, in great want and distress.'

His congregation, he wrote in February 1841, 'generally live on the poorest and scantiest fare, and many of them for a part of the year are supported mainly by shell-fish; that, by sending their families annually to the south to labour there, the parents are, to a certain extent, upheld; and that, when every other resource fails them, they live on their wealthier neighbours, some by begging, and some by stealing.'

Another crisis then affected the common people of Duirinish. Just as they were suddenly impoverished by the collapse of the kelp trade, so MacLeod of MacLeod found that his own income from the export of kelp ash had fallen drastically, and that as a consequence he had no further use for much of his tenantry.

MacLeod began to sell or lease large amounts of land. The MacLeods of Dunvegan had embarked on this procedure before and during the kelp boom. Their repossession of the MacCrimmon piping family's tied farm at Borreraig in 1770 was a small early manifestation. It and its surrounding acreage would later be sliced up and sold off as Husabost Estate. In 1789 General Norman, 23rd MacLeod of MacLeod, sold the island of Harris and its associated distant populated archipelago of St Kilda for £15,000 to Captain Alexander MacLeod, a sea-captain from the island of Berneray who had prospered in the East Indies trade. At Martinmas 1810 General Norman's son John Norman, the 24th chief, sold his 48,000 acres at Glenelg, a fertile and picturesque district on the Highland mainland close to Skye which had been in the family since 1540, to a London banker for the astonishing sum of £98,500, which would trans-late to roughly £5,000,000 early in the 21st century.

Equally pertinently to the people of Glendale, at the same time as the sale of Glenelg on the mainland, the MacLeods of Dunvegan were beginning to rent unprecedented quantities of their land to tacksmen, or tenant farmers. Tacksmen were not new to the Scottish Gaidhealtachd. As Dr Samuel Johnson noted in 1773: 'Next in dignity to the laird is the Tacksman; a large taker or lease-holder of land, of which he keeps part as a domain in his own hand, and lets part to under-tenants. The tacksman is necessarily a man capable of securing to the laird the whole rent, and is commonly a collateral relation. These tacks, or subordinate possessions, were long considered as hereditary, and the occupant was distinguished by the name of the place at which he resided. He held a middle station, by which the highest and the lowest orders were connected. He paid rent and reverence to the laird, and received them from the tenants. This tenure still subsists, with its original operation, but not with its primitive stability.'

Prior to the 20th century tacksmen had therefore been part of the established order of the Scottish Gaidhealtachd. They had almost always been of local families, Gaelic-speaking and often with a sense of social or clan responsibility. Like farmers in the south they employed labourers and servants, and their interests had not often been perceived as clashing with the interests of the lower orders. On the contrary, when large numbers of Highland tacksmen with some money in the bank joined 'the dance called America' and emigrated to the United States in the late 18th century, observers then and later mourned the departure from the glens and the islands of a Gaelic professional middle class which could have stabilised the region. 'As the mind must govern the hands,' wrote Dr Johnson, 'so in every society the man of intelligence must direct the man of labour. If the tacksman be taken away, the Hebrides must in their present state be given up to grossness and ignorance; the tenant, for want of instruction, will be unskilful, and for want of admonition, will be negligent.'

Far from all of the local Skye tacksmen went to North America. But those who remained quickly found their ranks augmented by rivalrous mainland farmers from the east and south of Scotland. Such men were usually unsentimental agricultural improvers, determined to make profitable what they saw as wasted acreage. They were frequently foreign to the region, unable even to converse with most of its Gaelic-speaking population, and indifferent to, if not scornful of, the Gaels' attachment to their birthplace and their modest aspirations.

It was and remained for many years contentious whether or not a Highland estate earned less money from the combined rent of, say, 300 crofters than from the single annual lease payment of one sheep farmer. But it was indisputably easier to administrate and collect one large lease payment than 300 small rents, especially if many or most of the 300 tenants were impoverished and liable to default.

Thus was established the dialectic of what became known as the Highland Land War. On the one hand lay the thesis proposed in 1841 by Reverend Archibald Clerk when writing about the Duirinish district of north-western Skye. As an Established Church of Scotland minister, Reverend Clerk owed his position to the landowner and was comfortable with the popular landowning view that Duirinish in particular and the Highlands in general were too small and bereft of natural resources to sustain their current population.

It must be evident 'to every thinking man,' wrote Reverend Clerk, 'that the main cause of the evil is to be found in the ignorance of the people themselves. Were they enlightened ... They would seek in other quarters of the world the means of independent and comfortable subsistence. They might fare much better where they are. But generally they are unenlightened – they are deplorably ignorant, and, being so, they are destitute of the true spirit of independence – of the proper ambition to better their circumstances. They feel a blind, and, therefore, a very powerful attachment to the rocks and glens amid which they were brought up – an almost invincible aversion to abandon them . . .

'The immediate and most obvious remedy for the evils arising from the superabundant population of the parish is confessedly the removing of numbers of the people, by emigration, to places where they may support themselves in comfort by the labour of their hands.

'This is a measure which is loudly called for by the circumstances of the country, – demanded more loudly and imperiously each succeeding year, – and a measure which, if now neglected, will speedily force itself on the notice both of the land-owners, and the government of the kingdom, not only by the piteous wailing of want and of famine, – not only by the sad spectacle of a once moral people becoming, through the hardening and animalizing influence of grinding poverty, the reckless slaves of low passions, – but by the still more alarming, though not more woeful, spectacle of a loyal and peaceable people giving themselves up to robbery and rapine. The flocks of the large sheepowners are annually thinned by those who feel the pinching of famine . . .'

On the other hand lay the growing belief of 'the people themselves' that their destitution was not caused by their own ignorance and unrealistic attachment to their 'rocks and glens'.

It was rather the result of too many of their glens being monopolised by sheep farmers while the crofters were left with too many rocks. Their solution was articulated in 1883 by a crofter from Glendale named John MacPherson. It was, he said, 'To give us the land, as there is plenty of it, and . . . we are quite willing to pay for it.'

John MacPherson's view was informed by his awareness that 'many of our landlords never purchased the properties which they have – that it was our forefathers who purchased the properties with their own blood, and that, therefore, we have as much right as anybody else to have it by purchase'. As for emigration to another country as an answer to land hunger, John MacPherson agreed, with one important qualification. 'I think it would be a capital thing,' he said 'for those [sheep farmers] who have the £1,800 tacks to go there, and then there would be no crofters in their way.'

That denial of the aristocracy's hereditary claim to the land, its sarcastic recommendation that the bourgeoisie rather than the common people should be deported and its belief in the equal distribution of land among the peasantry was, in the 19th century or at any other time, revolutionary. It was recognised as such by the authorities.

THREE

The Class System in Skye

IN THE LATE 1820s the Inspector of Highland Roads and Bridges, a young man from the north-eastern town of Forres named Joseph Mitchell, was overseeing in the parish of Bracadale the construction of one of those 'lines of excellent road' which were created almost everywhere in Skye but Glendale in the first half of the 19th century.

Mitchell noted, and remembered over 40 years later when he wrote his memoirs, that the Bracadale countryside was 'comparatively fertile'. He also knew that 'A year or two before it had been cleared of tenantry to the number of 1,500 souls . . . the ruined cottages and green spots of the once cultivated crofts were to be seen scattered on the hillside . . . But all was then a solitude, and nothing was heard by the passing traveller but the bleating of sheep.'

Bracadale is a large portion of Skye due east of Glendale. In the 1820s it belonged to the MacLeods of Dunvegan Castle. 'Where I was born, which was in Bracadale,' said a 55–year-old man in 1883, 'there were comfortable crofters there. They were in comfortable circumstances. They had cattle and sheep and horses. They had a great stretch of hill pasture.'

In the 1820s John Norman, the 24th chief who 15 years earlier had banked a small fortune from the sale of Glenelg, removed almost the entire population of the parish of Bracadale to create space for tenant sheep farmers.

Of the evicted families, 'all who could', according to one witness, 'went to America and other places'. Of the people who remained in Skye, 'those of them who were poorly, and could not flit and could not emigrate' were crowded into the shoreside Bracadale township of Coillore. Those who could not or would not emigrate but were healthy enough to flit were largely relocated at the other side of Loch Bracadale in Glendale.

They were moved around like so many herds of cattle, to 'wherever they could get a hole to live in'. Some of the Bracadale people were at first told to settle at Ramasaig and Lorgill on the rough south-western coast of Glendale, which was then still in the hands of MacLeod of MacLeod. They would later be evicted from Ramasaig and Lorgill to make room for a sheep ranch, and moved, like the last piping MacCrimmons, to Canada or to Fasach and other townships in Glendale. Some Bracadale families were sent further north, to the small populated hamlets of Upper and Lower Milovaig. Upper and Lower Milovaig had been themselves briefly cleared of people in 1840, to favour the same sheep farm, but the residents were permitted to return in 1845 in return for an increased annual rent. 'The same person,' wrote James Hunter in 2007, 'might find himself or herself made homeless over and over again.'

The results were unprecedented social instability and a dramatic overcrowding of certain parts of Glendale, both engineered by the same landowning interests which argued that Skye already contained far too many people for their own good. The cause and effect of that overcrowding in the microcosm of one crofting village was described in forensic detail in 1883 by John MacPherson, who had been born in Lower Milovaig in 1834. 'From time immemorial up till the year 1845,' said MacPherson, 'the township was tenanted by eight crofters, paying a rent of £7 each, or a total rental of £56.

'Each crofter kept six cows, a horse, and sixteen sheep; thereby living very comfortably, and buying very little of foreign produce, if any at all. At that time McLeod of McLeod was proprietor of this estate, as also of that of Bracadale, of which he is yet the proprietor; and by the evicting of the most of the tenants of Bracadale and Minginish, and also of many from other portions of McLeod's estates, in order to provide the evicted land for sheep farms, and also by the evicting of ten or a dozen from the estate of Major McDonald of Waternish, father of the present proprietor of that estate – the evicted land in this case being put under deer – the townships of Meiloveg (Upper and Lower) were overcrowded, as well as other townships on this estate.

'The division of the township into crofts was re-arranged, and instead of eight as formerly there were now seventeen crofts, and the rental was increased to about £80. These changes with regard to the Lower Meiloveg township was made in the year 1845; each crofter paid from £3 16s to £5.

'As may be supposed, the crofters were from the said changes only to hold three cows, eight sheep, and no horse. At present there are twenty crofts, or more properly seventeen crofts, and three of these subdivided, and two cottars. Our crofts produce only about one and a half times what we sow. My croft is about three acres of very shallow land, and the other crofters in my township of Lower Meiloveg have same amount of land and same quality. We and our wives do the ploughing and harrowing of our land, turning or tilling it with the cas-chrom [foot-plough], the most primitive mode of tilling I believe in existence.

'As the land does not get any rest, by leaving part of it uncultivated some years, it has been, as may be supposed, rendered very unproductive and poor. Our hill pasture has decreased in quantity and quality in proportion to the decrease of the amount and quality of our croft holding, from the following cause, viz., that formerly there were only eight families in Lower Meiloveg to cut peat from the hill ground (. . . our peats are cut on our hill pasture), whereas there are now twenty-two families cutting peat from the hill, so that it will be seen what amount of land this peat-cutting by twenty-two families since 1845 would take up, and besides the hill grazing is scarce enough for our cattle and sheep. And owing to this, they suffer badly, and instead of the milk they had formerly, now only treacle and tea to wash down the food; that is, if there be anything to buy the said commodities.

'We are frugal and not extravagant in our way of living, our staple food being meal, potatoes, fish when it is got, our only drink and beverage being tea. On an average, we consume about sixteen bolls of south country meal. Were it not for our potato crop the year it grows well, we would have no value in the crop, for which we pay so dear, with regard to what we make of meal.

'We have very miserable dwelling-houses, and never got aid from our proprietors to build better ones. They are thatched with straw; and as our crofts do not produce the required amount of straw necessary for fodder for the cattle and thatch for our houses, and as we are prohibited from cutting rushes or pulling heather by the proprietor, the condition of our dwelling-houses in rainy weather is most deplorable. Above our beds come down pattering the rain, rendered dirty and black by the soot on the ceiling above, through which, as has been shown, for want of thatch, the rain has free access, and in consequence the inmates of the beds have to look for shelter from the rain in some dry place on the lee side of the house. Of the twenty crofters' houses, there are only two in which the cattle are not under the same roof with the family. Now we leave it to [you] to see what this revelation of the condition of our dwellings reflects on the boasted civilisation of the nineteenth century.'

The conditions in Milovaig and other townships in Glendale were exacerbated by the monopoly of most of the west of the peninsula immediately adjacent to their crofts by one large private sheep run. After 1843 the 800 acres of Waterstein Farm – 'one of the finest grazings, or arable lands, in the Island' – were leased from MacLeod of MacLeod for £130, rising to £140 a year by a scion of one of the old tacksman families of

Skye, Dr Nicol Martin of Trotternish. Martin, who was born
in 1801, was both a Gaelic speaker and a General Practitioner
who had earlier bought from the MacLeods of Dunvegan the
5,000–acre Husabost estate in north Glendale, which contained
the piping MacCrimmons' farmland that had been repossessed
by MacLeod in 1770. Nicol Martin had then taken up residency
in Husabost House. In his own words, he supplied the people of
the district 'with medicine and medical advice so long as I was
able to visit their sick . . . I still continue to give medicine and
advice to all and sundry – every one who comes. I keep a stock
of medicine, and they all come to me for medicine and advice.'

Dr Nicol Martin nonetheless came to regard the crofters of
his native island with contempt. In his gouty old age, Martin
asserted that while the Glendale crofters' wives decked themselves out in 'boas and bonnets and feathers' and sold their eggs
for 'tea and sugar and tobacco', the direct consequence of their
indulgences was that their children were 'weakly, scrofulous,
and very much deteriorated'. Dr Martin's unoriginal remedy 'for
them is to go where they can get land – that is, America. Go to
Manitoba and various parts of America and Canada, and you
can get lands there very cheap'. He personally, said Dr Nicol
Martin, 'would give £500 today if all the crofters on my place
went away'.

For their part, the crofters of Glendale saw no good reason
to cross the Atlantic Ocean in search of land. They could see
all the land they required on Dr Martin's rented sheep farm at
Waterstein, as well as on his 5,000 acres at Husabost.

Despite such sales and leases to tenant farmers, in the late
1840s Norman, the 25th MacLeod of MacLeod, found himself
all but bankrupted. Luckily, ten years earlier he had made a
good marriage to Louisa Barbara St John, the daughter of the
Baron of Bletso. Norman leased out the dilapidated 500 year-
old Dunvegan Castle, put his Highland affairs into the hands
of his sister Emily and moved to pursue a civil service career in
London.

Five years later, in 1852, he also followed the examples set by his father and grandfather by slicing off another large piece of his hereditary Skye possessions and selling it to a wealthy southern purchaser. This time the large piece of Skye was the newly delineated 35,000 acres of Glendale estate, which ran from Lochs Dunvegan and Bracadale and the Brunigill burn to Neist and Idrigill Points, and took in all of the crofting settlements in between, from Skinidin and Colbost to Ramasaig and Lower Milovaig.

The wealthy purchaser of the new Glendale estate was one of the most curious of 19th-century Highland landowners. John MacPherson MacLeod had been born in Dunbartonshire in 1792. His father, Lieutenant-Colonel Donald MacLeod, was the scion of a Colbost tacksman family, some of whose male members had gained fame and fortune in the British Army and who had consequently been able to buy outright much of the land around Skinidin and Colbost. As an adult later in the 18th century Donald MacLeod himself maintained the tradition as an officer in the East Indian Army. That enabled him to add a small estate at Auchagoyle in Argyllshire to his family's property portfolio, and in 1804 to buy St Kilda from Alexander MacLeod, the Hebridean sea captain who had taken the islands off the hands of the 23rd MacLeod of MacLeod in 1789.

Upon the death in Edinburgh of Lieutenant-Colonel Donald MacLeod in 1813, his small property at Skinidin and Colbost and his significant archipelago of St Kilda (which was already celebrated as the most isolated populated landfall in the United Kingdom) were inherited by his 21-year-old son, John MacPherson MacLeod. The young man was initially unable to enjoy them. After graduating from Edinburgh University, John MacPherson MacLeod had been one of the first students to attend Haileybury College, a school established in Hertfordshire in 1806 by the East India Company specifically to train young men as 'writers', or administrators, in the Raj. (The East India Company was able to attract some notable instructors. John

MacPherson MacLeod's principal at Haileybury was the celebrated antiquarian and friend of Thomas Jefferson and Henry
Swinburne, Samuel Henley. His professor of political economy
was Thomas Malthus. He was taught mathematics by a future
Fellow of the Royal Society, William Dealtry.)

Following Haileybury, John MacPherson MacLeod went
straight to Madras, and in 1832 he became commissioner for
the Government of Mysore. For most of the rest of his life, with
the exception of one visit to Glendale, where he let his inherited
acreage at Colbost to tacksmen, his single experience of his
inherited Hebridean properties remained a voyage to St Kilda as a
12-year-old in 1804, the year of his father's purchase of the islands.

Five decades later, in the early 1850s, when he added almost
the whole of Glendale to his property portfolio, the 60 year-old
John MacPherson MacLeod was living with a butler, a footman,
a ladies' maid, a cook, a housemaid and his wife Catherine – an
Edinburgh woman from an elevated social background – in
an elegant town house in Stanhope Street, close to Hyde Park
in west London. He was semi-detached from the East India
Company and would soon retire from service. In recognition
of his Highland background and interests he had been made
an Inverness-shire magistrate and would shortly be raised to
Deputy Lord Lieutenant of the county. He was knighted by
Queen Victoria in 1866, and Sir John MacPherson MacLeod
was sworn into the Privy Council at Windsor Castle in 1871.

In 1857 the Edinburgh poet Alexander Smith married into this
Skye social milieu. Smith visited his wife's home in the south of
the island for each of the nine remaining summers of his life. He
became intimately familiar with the tacksman and landowning
classes. When he wrote a book about the island, *A Summer in
Skye*, Smith deployed pseudonyms and mingled identities. One of
those multiple personalities, which may or may not have included
aspects of John MacPherson MacLeod, was an example of the
Highland East India Company man based 'in the north-western
portion of the island' known as 'The Landlord'.

Alexander Smith's Skye Landlord 'had spent the best part of his life in India, was more familiar with huts of ryots, topes of palms, tanks in which the indigo plant was steeping, than with the houses of Skye cotters and the processes of sheep-farming.

'He knew the streets of Benares or Delhi better than he knew the streets of London; and, when he first came home, Hindostanee would occasionally jostle Gaelic on his tongue. The Landlord too, was rich, would have been considered a rich man even in the southern cities; he was owner of many a mile of moorland, and the tides of more than one far-winding Loch rose and rippled on shores that called him master.

'In my friend the Landlord there was a sort of contrariety, a sort of mixture or blending of opposite elements which was not without its fascination. He was in some respects a resident in two worlds. He liked motion; he had a magnificent scorn of distance: to him the world seemed comparatively small; and he would start from Skye to India with as much composure as other men would take the night train to London. He paid taxes in India and he paid taxes in Skye.

'His name was as powerful in the markets of Calcutta as it was at the Muir of Ord. He read the *Hurkaru* and the *Inverness Courier*. He had known the graceful salaam of the East, as he now knew the touched bonnets of his shepherds. And in living with him, in talking with him, one was now reminded of the green western island on which sheep fed, anon of tropic heats, of pearl and gold, of mosque and pinnacle glittering above belts of palm-trees. In his company you were in imagination travelling backwards and forwards. You made the overland route twenty times a day. Now you heard the bagpipe, now the monotonous beat of the tom-tom and the keen clash of silver cymbals. You were continually passing backwards and forwards, as I have said. You were in the West with your half-glass of bitters in the morning, you were in the East with the curry at dinner . . .'

It may have been relevant that in the early 1850s Norman, the 39–year-old 25th MacLeod of MacLeod, lived with his wife and young family and servants in similarly comfortable circumstances in Montagu Place, just a few streets and a few minutes' brisk walk from the Stanhope Street household of John MacPherson MacLeod. Norman had begun his career in the civil service and was then under-secretary to the Prison Board.

In the same year that he bought the expansive new Glendale estate from his clan chief and London neighbour MacLeod of MacLeod, John MacPherson MacLeod found himself with a disturbing problem in his other, inherited, property of St Kilda. In 1852 no fewer than 36 St Kildans, a third of the total population of 110 men, women and children, decided to emigrate to Australia. They set off for the port of Liverpool by way of Harris, Skye and then overland to Glasgow. Alerted to their departure, John MacPherson MacLeod hurried to meet them in Glasgow and accompanied them to Liverpool, pleading with them all along to return to St Kilda. The proprietor offered to charter a steamer to take them home, and then to 'give them all they needed for two years'. The St Kildans refused. By travelling as far south as Glasgow they had already stretched the umbilical cord to snapping point. 'We told him,' said one of them, 'probably the rest of the inhabitants would come away shortly.' John MacPherson MacLeod then relinquished any hope of sending his 36 former tenants back to St Kilda. He even paid the fare from Liverpool to Australia of those who were hard-pressed.

In the course of his discussions with the emigrating St Kildans, MacLeod was told unpleasant things about his factor. Norman MacRaild was a 47–year-old member of a small but established tacksman family at Colbost, by Glendale, who was familiar to John MacPherson MacLeod through MacLeod's own family's connections with the township. As the youngest brother of three, Norman had failed to inherit his father's ten-acre tack at Colbost, but had remained in Skye. In 1842 MacLeod, who was then still fully occupied in India, appointed Norman MacRaild as his factor, and de facto regent, to St Kilda.

According to the 36 emigrating St Kildans, MacRaild had

abused both them and his position. When, like most other Protestant Highlanders, the St Kildans left the Established Church of Scotland for the new Free Church of Scotland following the Disruption of 1843, Norman MacRaild refused to allow them to use the only church on their islands. 'He [MacRaild] was vexed at the state of matters,' said one St Kildan. 'He threatened to evict any who refused to go [back to the Established Church of Scotland].' Norman MacRaild, the St Kildans insisted to their concerned proprietor, 'had overstepped his powers'.

John MacPherson MacLeod immediately revoked Norman MacRaild's injunction against the remaining St Kildans using their church building and its manse, and within a few months a Free Church of Scotland missionary was settled there. MacLeod retained MacRaild as factor of St Kilda until he sold the islands in 1871, by which time Norman MacRaild was 68 years old and had taken the family's small farm at Colbost over from his older brother.

But for motives which are likely to have been influenced by the unhappy events in St Kilda between 1843 and 1852, despite the fact that Norman MacRaild had been born in Colbost and was his tacksman and ground officer there, John MacPherson MacLeod did not make MacRaild the factor of his new, much bigger estate of Glendale. After a couple of temporary appointments, MacLeod turned instead to another man. Ironically, he was the man whose activities, as much as those of any other individual, would provoke insurrection two decades later.

In the early 1860s, however, Donald MacDonald seemed an obvious choice as factor to Glendale estate. Donald MacDonald of Tormore, who would always be known throughout Skye and beyond after his place of origin as 'Tormore', was one of the most successful upper-middle-class tacksmen of his time. He was born in 1835 into an affluent landholding family at Tormore Farm, a sizeable piece of good earth close to Armadale Castle in the south-east of Sleat in the south of Skye, far away from Glendale, on the estate of Lord Macdonald, the High Chief of Clan Donald, to whom he was related. Donald's father, Alexander, was 46 years old when his 20–year-old wife Isabella gave birth to their first surviving child. There would be six other children, six brothers and sisters for Donald, and Isabella was helped in their upbringing by a governess and half-a-dozen household servants. The young Donald and his siblings were raised bilingually in their Gaelic-speaking environment, being tutored at home by an English-speaking Scottish Lowlander.

The Edinburgh man Alexander Smith would almost certainly have known Donald MacDonald in adulthood. The two were contemporaries – Smith was the older by six years – and Smith's wife Flora MacDonald was the daughter of another Sleat tacksman named Charles MacDonald, whose property, where Smith spent his summers, was five miles north of Tormore on the western side of the peninsula around Ord House. Alexander Smith was therefore more familiar with the tacksman generation of Tormore's father Alexander MacDonald and his own father-in-law Charles, which still in many cases held to Georgian values.

In affectionately describing Charles MacDonald of Ord House, Smith therefore offered a description of the old patriarchal society in which Donald MacDonald was raised, rather than the new materialistic Victorian polity in which Tormore was to thrive. '[MacDonald] had his own code of generous old-fashioned ethics,' wrote Alexander Smith, 'to which he steadily adhered; and the man who was hard on the poor, who would dream of driving them from the places in which they were born, seemed to him to break the entire round of the Commandments.

'Consequently the huts still smoked on the hem of the shore and among the clumps of birch-wood. The children who played on the green when he first became tacksman grew up in process of time, and married; and on these occasions he not only sent them something on which to make merry withal, but he gave them – what they valued more – his personal presence; and he made it a point of honour, when the ceremony was over, to dance the first reel with the bride . . .

'When required, Mr [MacDonald] demands the services of these people just as he would the services of his household servants, and they comply quite as readily. If the crows are to be kept out of the corn, or the cows out of the turnip-field, an urchin is remorselessly reft away from his games and companions. If a boat is out of repair, old Dugald is deputed to the job, and when his task is completed, he is rewarded with ten minutes' chat and a glass of spirits up at the house. When fine weather comes, every man, woman, and child is ordered to the hay-field, and Mr [MacDonald] potters amongst them the whole day, and takes care that no one shirks his duty. When his corn or barley is ripe the cotters cut it, and when the harvest operations are completed, he gives the entire cotter population a dance and harvest-home. But between Mr [MacDonald] and his cotters no money passes; by a tacit understanding he is to give them house, corn-ground, potato-ground, and they are to remunerate him with labour.

'Mr [MacDonald], it will be seen, is a conservative, and hates change; and the social system by which he is surrounded wears an ancient and patriarchal aspect to a modern eye. It is a remnant of the system of clanship. The relation of cotter and tacksman, which I have described, is a bit of antiquity quite as interesting as the old castle on the crag – nay, more interesting, because we value the old castle mainly in virtue of its representing an ancient form of life, and here is yet lingering a fragment of the ancient form of life itself. You dig up an ancient tool or weapon in a moor, and place it carefully in a museum: here, as it were, is the ancient tool or weapon in actual use.

'No doubt Mr [MacDonald's] system has grave defects: it perpetuates comparative wretchedness on the part of the cotters, it paralyses personal exertion, it begets an ignoble contentment; but on the other hand it sweetens sordid conditions, so far as they can be sweetened, by kindliness and good services. If Mr

[MacDonald's] system is bad, he makes the best of it, and draws as much comfort and satisfaction out of it, both for himself and for others, as is perhaps possible.'

That mirage would shortly evaporate once and for all in the hands of such heritors as Donald 'Tormore' MacDonald. Donald MacDonald would become the most successful of all the children of Alexander and Isabella MacDonald of Tormore Farm. He never married but remained throughout his life uxoriously wedded to ambition, property and status. By 1861, when he was in his mid-20s, he had replaced his dead father as head of his household, had taken over the family farm and was busily increasing its acreage by the acquisition of several other south Skye properties. He acquired a farm on the eastern mainland in Nairnshire. By 1871 the 35 year-old Donald MacDonald would describe himself as a 'farmer of 10,000 acres of which about 2,000 are arable – employing 11 shepherds and labourers'. He also became both a Justice of the Peace and an estate factor for Lord Macdonald of Sleat and other landowners in Skye and the neighbouring mainland.

In the spring of 1862 John MacPherson MacLeod asked the 26 year-old Donald MacDonald to become factor of his 35,000–acre Glendale estate. Donald 'Tormore' MacDonald was a natural choice. As his privileged boyhood suggests, he lay close in the Victorian social stratum to the aristocratic Highland gentry, and a very long way above the crofters, fishermen and cottars of Skye whose language he nonetheless shared. Tormore could and did communicate with all parties, but he was not a middleman. He liked many of the lower orders and many of them liked him. Although he exercised control over the minutiae of everyday commercial life on his estates, such as a monopoly of local cattle-dealing, he was regarded widely as a fair and honest man. A substantial body of tenants in Sleat would commend Tormore in writing as 'the people's best friend'. Tormore himself would say of his more northerly charges, 'We were on the very best of terms, and I can speak very kindly of the people of Glendale.' But he was ultimately answerable and sympathetic only to the landholding class, of which he was a cadet.

There is more than a hint of Tormore in one of Alexander Smith's supposed descriptions of 'the Landlord'. 'When he entered on the direction of his property,' wrote Smith, '[he] exploded every ancient form of usage, actually *ruled* his tenants; would permit no factor, middle-man, or go-between; met them face to face, and had it out with them. The consequence was that the poor people were at times sorely bewildered. They received their orders and carried them out, with but little sense of the ultimate purpose of the Landlord – just as the sailor, ignorant of the principles of navigation, pulls ropes and reefs sails and does not discover that he gains much thereby, the same sea-crescent being around him day by day, but in due time a cloud rises on the horizon, and he is in port at last.'

One of his fiercest and most persistent critics, Alexander MacKenzie, would write: 'Tormore, as a man, was a very good fellow, and one is sorry to find him placed in a position in which, by contact with a pernicious system, he not only becomes a changed man, but is, on occasions, driven to the commission of acts unworthy of a gentleman of his position and pretensions . . .

'Tormore, the factor, and Tormore, the man, are evidently two widely different persons. Indeed this is the case with most of his class. They have, in many instances, to do the dirty work of employers who would be perfectly ashamed and quite incapable of doing it for themselves, though they are not always ashamed to bask in the sunshine of society in the South on the proceeds of factorial meannesses and accumulated tyrannies on their neglected people and properties in the North.'

For as long as the lines of command and obeisance were recognised, Donald 'Tormore' MacDonald could be the people's friend. The moment those lines were questioned or even crossed, he became their implacable enemy.

FOUR

Tinder-boxes Waiting for a Spark

JOHN MACPHERSON was an almost exact contemporary of
Donald 'Tormore' MacDonald. MacPherson was born into
a world of uncertainty in Milovaig on 10 December 1834.
His mother Flora was a native of Pollosgan, a settlement within
stone's throw of Milovaig; his father Alexander had been born
a mile to the south in Waterstein. The Milovaig which John
MacPherson knew as a small boy was the township which he
later described as 'tenanted by eight crofters . . . Each crofter
kept six cows, a horse, and sixteen sheep; thereby living very
comfortably, and buying very little of foreign produce, if any at
all.'

The MacPhersons were already part of a noted Glendale
family. Flora MacPherson was a sister of the celebrated Skye
bard Donald MacLeod, 'Domhnall nan Oran', and an aunt of
two other scions of that poetic family, Neil MacLeod and Iain
'Dubh' MacLeod. Flora's and Donald's father had a small farm
in Glendale and was able to educate his children to the extent
that they were unusually literate in both Gaelic and English.
(Donald published his first Gaelic poems in 1811, when he was
just 24 years old and well known throughout Skye as a collector
of road rates.)

Their family's erudition and renown did not insulate them
from the harshnesses of the time. When Milovaig was forcibly
emptied in 1840 to make room for a small rented sheep farm,

Alexander and Flora MacPherson and their four young children – eight year-old Margaret, five year-old John, three year-old Donald and the toddler Neil – were moved across the Glendale valley to the township of Lephin at the east of the bridge over the Hamara River.

When Milovaig was repopulated in 1845 the MacPherson family, which by then included two more infant sons, was given a four-acre let, or croft, back in Lower Milovaig. The village was simultaneously swollen by other immigrants from elsewhere in north-western Skye. The number of crofts on that small piece of thin earth was more than doubled from eight to seventeen. The number of cows and sheep permitted to each crofting household was correspondingly halved to three and eight respectively, and nobody was allowed to keep a horse. The large neighbouring district of Waterstein, where Alexander MacPherson had been born and bred and which had in earlier times been common land, was let as a sheep farm to Dr Nicol Martin and declared out of bounds to crofters.

Then, when John MacPherson of Lower Milovaig was 11 years old, came the potato blight of 1846 and the famines of succeeding years. In common with their Celtic cousins in Ireland, by the middle of the 19th century Hebridean crofters had become disproportionately dependent on the potato. Ironically, John's uncle Donald MacLeod had earlier written a light verse titled 'Òran a Bhuntata', 'Song in Praise of the Potato'. Among its many other qualities, Domhnall nan Oran had rhapsodised, the potato was a generous source of nutrition whose dependability was superior to that 'brother to famine', traditional barley or oatmeal 'thin' porridge.

The blight was a trans-European phenomenon. In the year of 1845 it had destroyed between 70 and 90 per cent of potato crops in the Low Countries. It arrived in the Scottish Highlands with heavy rain in July 1846 and by the end of that autumn it was estimated that Skye had lost 80 per cent of its potato yield. It was a traumatic event. There would be other, smaller crop failures in following decades, but the late 1840s would be remembered as the period when a staple foodstuff rotted in the ground and neither the crop nor the people ever properly recovered. 'Poverty was increasing,' said a 70 year-old north Skye crofter 35 years after the event, 'ever since the potatoes began to fail at first.'

In the family legend of MacLeod of MacLeod, the clan chief's ruin was also completed by the great potato famine. When it began Norman, the 24th chief, was 34 years old, in the eleventh year of his suzerainty, and married with a young family in Dunvegan Castle. He and his Bedfordshire wife had made sterling efforts to convert the interior and the gardens of their medieval keep into a home fit for 19th-century aristocrats. They also made inefficient attempts to farm some of MacLeod's remaining Skye properties. When the potato famine struck in 1846, wrote his great-great-grand-daughter-in-law in the following century, 'Without hesitation, the young chief sold his private fortune with all his possessions, including pictures, plate and furniture, and with the money paid for road-making, bridge-building and drainage . . . Some help came from outside, but very little. Norman MacLeod spent from £225 to £300 a week, and in 1847 he wrote in a letter that he was feeding between six and seven thousand people. His personal resources could not long stand up to this burden, but he wrote, "Ruin must be faced rather than let the people die." Never once did he question where his duty lay, nor what a landlord and chief must do for his people. They owed him their lives, but when the famine ended he was totally ruined.'

That account has an understandable familial bias. In fact the whole of the Highlands and Islands received a large amount of 'help from outside'. In contrast to the contemporaneous disaster in Ireland, churches, lay organisations and the British Government organised, subsidised and distributed substantial famine relief, chiefly in the form of ground meal, to the stricken Highlands. In February 1847 the three most prominent

Highland relief committees, one in Edinburgh, one in Glasgow and one established by the four-year-old Free Church of Scotland, were combined in the Government-assisted Central Board of Management for Highland Relief. The Highland Relief Board organised its own job creation schemes, such as road-building, in return for assistance, and landowners such as MacLeod of MacLeod were informed by the Government that they were expected to do the same.

Whether or not he spent the substantial sum of £300 a week feeding up to 7,000 people, Norman MacLeod's efforts were therefore neither unique nor entirely voluntary. Nor was his 'total' ruination remotely comparable to the condition of his tenants. He found himself living in an elegant townhouse in the west end of London with two maids and a governess for his children. Despite his lack of educational qualifications (Norman MacLeod had attended Harrow School but had failed to progress from there to university) his position and social connections parachuted him into a salaried position in the civil service.

At the same time, John MacPherson was crowded with his parents and seven siblings in a thatched two-roomed blackhouse in Lower Milovaig. The children did have a cursory education. They owed their literacy in Gaelic and their fluency in English to their exceptional parents and to their occasional attendance at the Glendale Sabbath church school. All of the MacPherson children could write at least their own names, which was not commonplace in the mid-19th-century Scottish Gaidhealtachd, and John was able to read in Gaelic and English. The 16-year-old John and his 14-year-old brother Donald had to become fishermen in the wild waters of Uist Sound to supplement their parents' labours on the four-acre croft. By dint of backbreaking work with a hand-held plough and a peat iron and by hauling longlines from the open sea, the MacPhersons did not starve.

Nor, unlike many of their relatives, neighbours and fellow islanders, were the MacPhersons forced to leave Skye for

Glasgow, North America or Australasia. Emigration, the panacea prescribed for them by so many following the collapse of the kelp trade, was forced upon tens of thousands of Highlanders and Hebrideans by the potato famine. Between 1841 and 1881 the population of Skye fell from 23,000 to 16,800. In the same four decades the population of the parish of Duirinish, including Glendale, collapsed from around 5,000 to fewer than 3,000 people.

Those 3,000 people, like most of the other 14,000 survivors in Skye, would prove to be battered and bruised but unbroken.

In 1862, when Donald 'Tormore' MacDonald became the factor of John MacPherson MacLeod's Glendale estate, the 26–year-old John and 24–year-old Donald MacPherson were still working as fishermen. Their father Alexander had died, and their 61–year-old mother Flora was helped on the croft by her 19–year-old son Alexander.

Three years later, in March 1865, John MacPherson married. It was a historically significant match in that he married into, and thereby became intimately familiar with the recent history of, one of the families which had been cleared from Bracadale. Margaret MacLean had been born in Bracadale 25 years earlier, and as an infant had been forcibly removed from the new sheep ranch there to Glendale with her parents Norman and Mary MacLean. The MacLeans resettled in Fasach until Margaret's marriage to John at Glendale Church of Scotland, after which she moved into the Lower Milovaig household of the MacPherson family. Her husband John then gave up the dangerous sea and moved onto the land, taking over husbandry of the family croft.

In the course of the next ten years Margaret MacPherson presented John with two daughters and three sons. In January 1876 she died in Lower Milovaig of a fever at the age of 36 years.

Eighteen months later John MacPherson married again, to a 38–year-old widow from Feriniquarrie named Mary

MacDonald. Mary MacPherson took over the care of John's five children and added two of her own. That is where they stood in 1881: still at Number 10 Lower Milovaig, with two daughters in their early teens who helped Mary about the house and in her crofting duties, and three sons between seven and eleven years old who all attended the new local Board School. John MacPherson was 44 years old and Mary MacPherson was 40 years old. The tenor of their lives, which had not been uneventful, was about to change dramatically.

The middle-aged John MacPherson had become an impressive character. In 1883 a reporter for the *Inverness Courier* described him as 'a man of striking appearance, bold and manly bearing, great intelligence, and considerable mental power . . .' Three years later in 1886, when MacPherson had achieved national renown, a visitor to the Highlands met him in Milovaig. 'The men of Glendale are, without doubt, the finest-looking fellows I have come in contact with,' the visitor would write. 'The majority are tall and broad-shouldered. They are industrious, well-clothed, and courteous to strangers. John Macpherson . . . is a good type of the average Glendale-man. He is a broad-shouldered, hardy-looking Celt, with a bushy brown beard, just tinged with grey. His forehead betokens considerable brain-power, his eyes are brimful of intelligence, and his hard-set chin and firm lips denote decision of character . . . He is about fifty years of age, and was born in the township of Milivaig, Glendale, where he has been a crofter for thirty years. He belongs to a talented family, being a nephew of Donald Macleod . . . known as the "Skye Bard", and having several relatives holding good positions in the South . . . He is married, and has seven of a family, most of whom bid fair to inherit the patriotic feelings and ability of their father.'

By 'patriotic feelings' the writer was referring neither to British nor to Scottish nationalism. He meant that John MacPherson had a deep attachment to his Highland Celtic heritage and mili-tant convictions about the rights and aspirations of his fellow

Gaels. By the last third of the 19th century he was far from being the only Scottish Gael to possess such sentiments. He was simply the most famous of them all.

John MacPherson's generation grew up in hunger, insecurity and depopulation. Those dark riders formed its character. MacPherson and his contemporaries devoted themselves to ensuring that their grandchildren would face a better world. By the start of the 20th century, when they were either old or dead, they had largely succeeded.

If the century between the defeated Jacobite Rising of 1745 and 1746 and the post-famine emigrations of the 1850s and 1860s marked the nadir of Gaelic Scotland, the decades which followed featured a revitalisation which had come to seem impossible. It was focused on the most precious and apparently irrecoverable of all of the Gaels' native assets: the land.

No one date can be given to the time when Highlanders lost their land. It was, in Glendale as elsewhere, a piecemeal process which occurred over decades. The great-grandchildren of an 18th-century clansman found themselves, almost without having noticed the process, stripped of their ancestor's common rights to pastures and arable patches, and even of their homes. That was the experience of the young John MacPherson in the years after the clearance of Milovaig in 1840, and it was the experience of tens of thousands elsewhere.

The Glasgow Liberal MP and proprietor of the *North British Daily Mail*, Dr Charles Cameron MP, would summarise their position in a speech given at Liverpool to the Federation of Celtic Societies early in 1883. 'Before the '45 rising,' said Cameron, 'the tenants in the Highlands had distinct proprietary rights on the land they cultivated, and the chiefs were looked upon as the trustees for the clans. But after '45 the feudal system was introduced, the tenants lost their rights, and the landlords were made the absolute proprietors of the land.

'In Scotland there was provision made for the registration of titles to land; but the very existence of that registration had the effect of quickly getting rid of the proprietary interests of the tenants. The landlords, of course, registered their titles, but the crofters knew nothing about the system of registration, and took no trouble to register the rights they had in the land.' As the title of a 21st-century book on Scottish land ownership would summarise, the poor had no lawyers.

No single year can claim the start of the fightback, but a decade may be apportioned some credit. In the 1870s a number of exceptional Highlanders, both in exile and at home, began to develop a political awareness of their people's recent history, a consequent political realisation of their current plight, and a political programme for radical change. In 1871 John MacPherson's usually placid and apolitical maternal cousin, the 28-year-old Neil MacLeod, who had left Glendale six years earlier, would write at his new home in Edinburgh:

'Tha na Gaidheil air claonadh om maise . . .'

'The Gaels have declined in their fineness
and have yielded to weakness in many matters:
the rule of their land and country
they have handed to people with no right to it . . .'

Something was afoot.

In the summer of 1873 a new magazine was published in Inverness. 'From one end of the country to the other,' the magazine editorialised, 'there are complaints in regard to the land. There is not a district in which the evils of a defective land system are not complained of. From within a short distance of the Pentland Firth, a voice reaches us, that the people have been swept off the land, and that the soil is not made to yield its proper increases.

'From the straths of Sutherland, from the mountain sides of Ross-shire, and from the glens of Inverness-shire, Argyllshire, and Perthshire, much the same sound reaches us; from Kintail,

Lochalsh and Lochcarron; from Glenelg, Lochaber, and Badenoch; from Strathspey, Strathdearn, and Strathnairn; from the Islands of Uist, Barra, Skye, Raasay, Mull, Islay, and Arran there is a wonderful concord of testimonies to the effect that wrong has been done to the people, and less inflicted on the nation as a whole, by the manner in which the land is administered.'

The magazine was called *The Highlander*, and its editor was a man named John Murdoch. Murdoch had been born in Nairnshire in north-eastern Scotland in 1818, but when he was nine years old his family moved to the island of Islay. Although he would later work in the industrialised Scottish Lowlands, in Lancashire, in Dublin and in Shetland before retiring as an excise officer in Inverness, that short Hebridean boyhood shaped John Murdoch's legacy. In his later years he became, in the words of the *Glasgow Weekly*, a tireless advocate of 'the cause of the people, and particularly the right of the Gaelic people to their native soil'. *The Highlander* was forced to cease publishing in 1882. It may not have survived to celebrate its greatest achievements, but by 1882 its work was effectively done.

John Murdoch was also a member of the Gaelic Society of Inverness, which had been established in 1871. In common with many of its equivalent Highland and Island associations in Glasgow, Edinburgh and London, the Inverness Gaelic Society became increasingly interested and involved in the land question as the 1870s turned into the dramatic 1880s. Other publications which came out of the melange of mainly professional Highland exiles, such as the *Celtic Monthly* and the *Celtic Magazine*, slowly introduced politics and the issue of land reform to their standard menu of Gaelic verse, scholarship and mythology. The weekly *Oban Times*, 'the Highlander's Bible', which had been founded in 1861, became within 20 years a firm advocate of the 'crofters' cause'. The 1872 Education Act provided mandatory schooling for all Scottish children between the ages of five and thirteen. The 1872 Act failed to provide for education in Gaelic, for which omission it has been criticised ever since. But following the Free

Church of Scotland schools which had been established across the Protestant Highlands since the 1840s, it did create a generation of Highlanders who were newly and almost universally literate in English, and therefore able to absorb the content of publications such as *The Highlander* and the *Oban Times*.

There had been an Irish National Land League since 1879. There was a National Land League of Great Britain in 1881. There would be an English and a Scottish Land Restoration League in 1884 (the word 'restoration' was a 19th-century synonym for 'nationalisation'). Each of those organisations, with their many splinter groups, was a formal manifestation of long-standing unrest. The manifesto of the English Land Restoration League summarised that unrest in the words: 'And whereas the appropriation to the few of the land on which and from which the people of England must live is an efficient cause of dulness of trade, lowness of wages, the idleness of men who should be at work, the forcing of women and children to unnatural toil, the depopulation of agricultural districts, the crowding of city slums, the sapping of national strength by forced emigration, the physical and mental deterioration due to unwholesome employment and lodgings, and of the vice and crime that spring from poverty:

'It is therefore the duty of all Englishmen to secure the restoration of England to its true owners, the people of England.'

John Murdoch knew of – and supported – the land leagues throughout the component nations of the United Kingdom. But his time as an exciseman in Dublin had put him in close contact with such pillars of the Irish organisation as Michael Davitt. The political and cultural similarities between rural Ireland and the north-west of Scotland were inescapable. There would not yet be an official Highland Land League, but throughout the later 1870s a number of Scottish Highlanders and their comrades acted as though it already existed.

The Irish connection was boosted by Hebridean men fishing off the coast of County Cork and Irish men fishing in the Minch (associations between Irish insurgents and Hebridean Gaels, especially those from the Roman Catholic islands of South Uist and Barra, had concerned the Edinburgh establishment since late in the 18th century). It was assisted by the fact that they all spoke different dialects of the same Celtic language. But it was chiefly promoted by the potato blight and famines of the late 1840s and 1850s, which had prompted tens of thousands of Highlanders and Irish people to travel south and east respectively to gather in the industrial melting pot of the Scottish Central Belt. There, the Gaelic cousins from different islands were often met with an antipathy that could only emphasise their shared predicament. 'The Celtic race is an inferior one,' said the *Fifeshire Journal* in 1851. ' . . . [E]migration to America is the only available remedy for the miseries of the race, whether squatting listlessly in filth and rags in Ireland, or dreaming in idleness and poverty in the Highlands and Islands of Scotland.'

Edward McHugh, who would become another friend and associate of John Murdoch and also, in due course, of John MacPherson of Lower Milovaig, personified the link.

McHugh was born into a Catholic, Irish-speaking family of smallholders in County Tyrone in 1853. In 1861, when Edward was eight years old, his family joined the exodus from rural Ireland to the Scottish Lowlands, where his father found work as a labourer in Greenock. Ten years after their emigration, in his late teens, Edward McHugh moved from Greenock to Glasgow and qualified as a compositor. There, in the words of his biographer Andrew Newby, McHugh's 'interest in political and economic issues flourished'.

McHugh would come to realise, not least through his friendship with John Murdoch, that the radical politics of Glasgow and even of Ireland were not exactly concurrent with the nascent demands of Scottish Highlanders. Highland radicalism would take many different directions in the years to come, from socialism to Home Rule to pan-Celtic nationalism to Liberal reformism. In the 1870s, when Edward McHugh was involving himself in left-wing Scottish politics, few Highland crofters were interested in much more than what was known as 'the three Fs'. Very far from 'restoration', or wholesale nationalisation of the land, most Scottish Gaels who remained in the Highlands merely wanted their private landlords to be obliged to behave with a degree of respect and responsibility. This could practically be achieved by legislating for fair rents, fixity of tenure as long as those rents were paid, and the crofter's freedom to sell his home, tenancy and improvements. In the words of a Glendale man, 'we would humbly pray for relief: 1. Fixity of tenure; 2. Enlarged holdings; 3. Fair rent fixed by law courts; 4. Compensation [upon sale or transfer of tenure, for improvements made by crofters to the land and holdings]; 5. Power to buy holdings similar to other nations.'

Along with the redistribution to the people of land recently let to large sheep farmers, that agenda was largely considered by Highlanders to be sufficient to return the security, ordinary dignity and freedom from want which had been stolen from them over the previous hundred years. The three Fs could only be achieved by parliamentary legislation. In the short term, the assuagement of land hunger, particularly when it was aggravated by the removal by factors of yet more pastureland from an already desperate and declining people, would be the catalyst for direct action.

Before McHugh, Murdoch or any of the land leagues came along, there were clear signs that Highland Gaels were prepared to settle their simmering grievances with their own bare hands. In 1874 a sheriff officer from Stornoway in the island of Lewis visited the westerly offshore island of Bernera to serve, on behalf of the landowner's factor, summonses of removal from some disputed grazing land to 58 crofters. In a foreshadow of things to come, Sheriff Officer Colin MacLennan was accompanied by the local estate's ground officer. They served their summonses, but before leaving Bernera MacLennan and his colleague were assaulted by children throwing clods of earth and by a group of adults who tore MacLennan's coat in a scuffle.

Upon his return to Stornoway Colin MacLennan filed complaints of assault against three Bernera men. The police arrested one of the men who happened to be in Stornoway, but an angry crowd came to his aid and it took the officers four hours to manhandle their suspect one hundred yards through Stornoway town centre to the police station. At subsequent hearings at Stornoway Sheriff Court all three of the Bernera men were acquitted, but Sheriff Officer Colin MacLennan was himself found guilty of assault.

More crucially, the interdicts against use of the grazings were allowed to lapse. The Bernera crofters kept their land. It was a whiff of grapeshot that echoed around the Highlands and Islands of Scotland.

In Glendale by the 1870s, the tone of Donald 'Tormore' MacDonald's factorship and the lease of Waterstein to Dr Nicol Martin's sheep farm were beginning to rankle. The overcrowded villagers of Milovaig and elsewhere saw their residual hill grazings deteriorate annually by increased peat-cutting – 'As the land does not get any rest, by leaving part of it uncultivated some years, it has been, as may be supposed, rendered very unproductive and poor. Our hill pasture has decreased in quantity and quality in proportion to the decrease of the amount and quality of our croft holding, from the following cause, viz., that formerly there were only eight families in Lower Meiloveg to cut peat from the hill ground (. . . our peats are cut on our hill pasture), whereas there are now twenty-two families cutting peat from the hill, so that it will be seen what amount of land this peat-cutting by twenty-two families since 1845 would take up, and besides the hill grazing is scarce enough for our cattle and sheep.'

Over at the other side of the hill they saw hired shepherds driving herds of Nicol Martin's blackfaced sheep across large pristine acreages of Waterstein. Glendale fishermen ordinarily, from preference, landed their small skiffs near their homes on the shore of Loch Pooltiel on the northern coast of the peninsula. But during strong north winds, which blew fiercely down the channel of Loch Pooltiel, they were accustomed to tying up instead below the sheltered south coast of Waterstein, and then walking home. The fishermen were peremptorily banned from this coastline of the sheep farm – 'We live in the wildest part of coast from the Mull of Cantyre [Kintyre] to Cape Wrath, and when returning from our nets in the Uist Channel we were prohibited from landing on the lee side, that is when the wind blew so that we could not land in Loch Poultiel, below our houses. We were not allowed to land our boats on the Waterstein side . . . we were obliged to do it [land at Waterstein], otherwise we would be in danger of drowning . . . but he [the factor, Tormore] ordered, in these notices, the shepherds to give us up to the law . . . for landing at all . . . We don't know very well, but we understood it meant a prohibition to us to go ashore at Waterstein at all, and walk over the hill to the [north] shore.'

After a period of growing ill-will between the estate and the sheep farmer and the inhabitants, the Glendale crofters were forbidden to own working dogs. That was apparently because they had used their dogs mischievously on Nicol Martin's Waterstein land, to harry Martin's flocks or to drive their own across the boundary. The ban on dogs was by the 1870s and 1880s a common injunction against crofters on the margins of leased sheep farms in Skye. Everywhere, in Glendale no less than in Sconser, Braes and Broadford where it also applied, it was clearly both an insult and an injury to crofters who still had their own small numbers of sheep to raise and who were naturally attached to their dogs.

When a Waterstein estate shepherd reported that a crofter's dog had killed one of his sheep – something which was denied by the Glendale crofters – matters became more serious. Alexander Ross of Fasach, a middle-aged crofter, accused the factor Tormore of 'ways and means he devised for killing the dogs we had for herding our flocks; in particular, the placing of

poisoned eggs and poisoned doses about our dwelling places . . .
I myself saw some of [the dogs] dying . . . poisoned eggs were
placed within sixty or eighty yards of the house of my neighbour,
and the poisoned doses also. The poisoned doses were like little
rolls of meat with poison laid in them.'

His own dog, said Alexander Ross, had not been poisoned
but had been shot dead by Tormore's estate gamekeeper. The
keeper, said Ross 'shot him with his gun in the well, and the
well is dry since then, although it was one of the best wells in
the country before then, but since then it has denied water . . .
My dog was following my wife, and she was coming home from
my brother's house to her own house, and the dog following her.
The dog was lapping the water of the well, and there he was shot
. . . I do not know what he did to the well; but likely if he could
kill the well, he would do it . . . I cannot judge a factor's heart by
the heart of any man.' Following this incident Alexander Ross
pursued an action against the gamekeeper in Portree Sheriff
Court, for killing his dog and firing a gun in the direction of his
wife. The keeper was found guilty and fined ten shillings. One
of Ross's neighbours and witnesses at Portree Sheriff Court was
shortly afterwards 'warned to remove' by Tormore, although 'I
know he was not in [rent] arrears'.

Ultimately, Donald 'Tormore' MacDonald won a legal
injunction which banned all crofters from setting foot on any
part of Waterstein, or upon the entire west coast of Glendale.
The magazine editor and author Alexander MacKenzie reported
that the following written warning was put up in 'the most
public part of the district', the Glendale post office:

Notice. – Whereas parties are in the habit of trespassing on the
lands of Glendale, Lowergill, Ramasaig, and Waterstein, in
searching and carrying away drift timber, notice is hereby given
that the shepherds and herds on these lands have instructions
to give up the names of any persons found hereafter on any part
of said lands, as also anyone found carrying away timber from

the shore by boats or otherwise, that they may be dealt with according to law. – Factor's Office, Tormore, 4th January, 1882.

Then there was the vexed matter of the shops. In around 1878 Tormore, who had established his own meal store in the district, decided to levy an additional rent on shopkeepers in Glendale. He put up notices in the district informing everybody of this fact. In his own words five years later, 'in the small district of Glendale, which though small is a very populous district, the small shops were becoming a nuisance. In every township there were four, five, or six shops. There was a good deal of shebeening going on. The people bartered a good deal, giving their eggs and other produce to go south, and getting whisky in return. This was considered by the proprietor and myself to be very injurious to the district, and I put up a notice, – which, I may say generally, was put up more to keep people in order than as necessarily to be acted upon, – that any one opening a shop would be charged an increase of £2.' In another version of the incident, which was never specifically denied by Tormore, the notice of surcharge went much further and would also be imposed upon any crofter who was known to be a patron of an unauthorised shop.

Donald MacDonald would later state that the threat of extracting an extra £2 a year had worked as a deterrent and that the money was never taken from Glendale shopkeepers or their customers. He was probably correct about the deterrence. Alexander MacKenzie wrote in 1883, 'At one time there were some small shops in Glendale, but these would appear to have practically vanished ... No one, however, appears to have ever been asked to pay this [extra £2], but the shops ceased to exist!' In an overcrowded place where crofting rents were already between £3 10 shillings and £5 a year for inadequate little patches of land, the shop surcharge was regarded as an act of petty tyranny or worse – it was suspected that Tormore was preparing to monopolise for himself the local retail trade, as he had been accused of doing at the other end of Skye in Sleat, and as he already monopolised control over virtually every other commercial activity in Glendale.

At the other side of Cnoc an t-Sìthein in Colbost the MacRaild family continued, on behalf of and unchecked by the estate, to exercise their own petty despotism. Almost a century and a half later Allan Campbell, who was born in the township in 1948, would relate: 'My grandfather Allan Campbell (Ailean Alasdair Dhòmhnaill) was born in Colbost in 1877 and he died in 1969, aged 93, and apart from the last two years of his life he was an exceptionally fit and strong man. Ailean Alasdair was also an accomplished seanchaidh [tradition bearer] . . .

'When he was about three years old – probably about 1880 – his mother and a neighbour had taken their young children to the shore to gather winkles to make an evening meal for their families. My grandfather recalled how the local factor Norman MacRaild came out of his house which was a short distance away, and how he stalked backwards and forwards above the beach, beating a cane against his leather boots.

'He remembered climbing up the beach holding his mother's hand while she carried the bucket of shellfish in the other, and how MacRaild was waiting for them at high water mark. The women lowered their buckets when he spoke to them. He was shouting, "Don't you know that this is my shellfish and that you are stealing!" and he kicked over the buckets and scattered the shellfish into the shingle with his boots. "Clear off home before I have the law on you!"

'Ailean Alasdair told how the women grabbed their children by the hands and ran sobbing with fear and shame – and he remembered that he and the other children were also crying with confusion and fright. Many years have passed since I last heard my grandfather tell of that incident but I will never forget the extraordinary rage which consumed him when he told the story. As I said the incident probably happened in 1880 – but almost 90 years later the memory was as painfully barbaric as ever.'

Such grievances large and small were not confined to Bernera in Lewis and Glendale in Skye. They were festering all over the north and west of Scotland. They erupted into physical revolt in Skye early in the 1880s for a number of reasons, including the facts that Skye was most affected by sheep farm leasing and that its population had been severely depleted even by Highland standards. In the 40 years between 1841 and 1881 Skye had lost 27 per cent of its population. No ordinary family in the island was not gravely affected by emigration and the absence, frequently the permanent absence in America or Australasia, of sons, daughters, brothers, sisters and often whole households of neighbours who left behind only their open bibles within the empty walls and beneath the decaying thatch of what had recently been a warm and busy home.

For all of his familial and friendly associations with the Skye landholding classes, the Lowlander Alexander Smith was able to sympathise, however sentimentally, with that sense of loss. 'Emigration is more painful to the Highlander than it is to the Englishman – this poet and painter have instinctively felt – and in wandering up and down Skye you come into contact with this pain, either fresh or in reminiscence, not unfrequently,' wrote Smith.

'Although the member of his family be years removed, the Skyeman lives in him imaginatively – just as the man who has endured an operation is for ever conscious of the removed limb. And this horror of emigration – common to the entire Highlands – has been increased by the fact that it has not unfre-quently been a forceful matter, that potent landlords have torn down houses and turned out the inhabitants, have authorised evictions, have deported the dwellers of entire glens.

'That the landlords so acting have not been without grounds of justification may in all probability be true. The deported villagers may have been cumberers of the ground, they may have been unable to pay rent, they may have been slowly but surely sinking into pauperism, their prospect of securing a comfortable subsistence in the colonies may be considerable, while in their own glens it may be nil, – all this may be true; but to have your house unroofed before your eyes, and made to go on board a ship bound for Canada, even although the passage-money be paid for you, is not pleasant.

'An obscure sense of wrong is kindled in heart and brain. It is just possible that what is for the landlord's interest may be for yours also in the long run; but you feel that the landlord has looked after his own interest in the first place. He wished you away, and he has got you away; whether you will succeed in Canada is matter of dubiety. The human gorge rises at this kind of forceful banishment – more particularly the gorge of the banished!'

What was more, those who remained could observe that depopulation was continuing apace. Within another 20 years Skye said farewell to another 3,000 people, a further 20 per cent of its population. Late-19th-century Skye men and women could see their proud island civilisation disappearing before their eyes, within their own lifetimes. Many of the island's remaining crofters were rack-rented, and their factors consequently marked most highly on a scale which ran from insensitive to brutal.

Many of Skye's crofting communities therefore became small tinder-boxes waiting for a spark. There were agitations, civil unrest and strikes all over Great Britain in the troubled 1880s. The Hebridean island of Skye was about to become, for a brief period, the nation's epicentre of agrarian revolution.

FIVE

Disturbances in the Braes

THE SPARK KINDLED in Kilmuir in 1881. Kilmuir estate contained most of the northern Skye peninsula of Trotternish: a spectacular single finger of land whose elevated spine, the Trotternish Ridge, rolled down to crofted foothills in the east and good green land in the west.

Kilmuir was the property of a career army officer from a landed east-coast family named William Fraser. Fraser had bought Kilmuir estate in 1855 from Lord Macdonald of Sleat, High Chief of the Clan Donald, in much the same kind of exchange from hereditary clan title to private commercial interest as had occurred when MacLeod of MacLeod sold such assets as Glendale to John MacPherson MacLeod.

William Fraser and his local tacksman factor Alexander Macdonald would have preferred to empty all of Kilmuir estate, from the townships around Staffin in the east to those between Uig and Duntulm in the west, and lease it either as one huge sheep ranch-cum-sporting estate, or as a smaller number of large sheep farms. The years of mass eviction were, however, coming to an end, and the two men satisfied themselves with letting only a couple of sheep farms in Trotternish. In an unashamed, and openly confessed, attempt to persuade Kilmuir tenants to leave voluntarily, as well as to improve the estate's finances, they satisfied themselves by rack-renting the remaining crofters. As in Glendale, the burden was increased further by the estate's transfer to the sheep farms of what had been common hill pasture.

Naturally enough, like Donald 'Tormore' MacDonald and Nicol Martin in Glendale, William Fraser and Alexander MacDonald did not regard themelves as oppressors. They were improvers. William Fraser was a committed member of the Inverness-shire Liberal Association. They considered that the island of Skye had been made economically unviable by its inefficient and bankrupt clan chieftains. Their mission was to get the place into the black. They recognised that this required regular doses of harsh medication, but they were equally convinced that posterity would eventually smile upon their efforts. In William Fraser's own words to Alexander MacDonald in 1877, 'I think it would be a mistake to allow the [crofters'] rents to continue at their present low rate, which indirectly seems to encourage a want of industry. The present state of croft agriculture throughout Kilmuir is very far back but with an increase of the rents it will become necessary to those who wish to continue to improve their lands a little.'

'I have built a school-house for them,' said Alexander Smith's composite 'Landlord' of the people on his north Skye estate in the 1860s, '. . . I have built a shop, as you see, a smithy, and a mill. I have done everything for them, and I insist that, when a man becomes my tenant, he shall pay me rent. If I did not so insist I should be doing an injury to myself and to him. The people on the hill-side pay me rent; not a man Jack of them is at this moment one farthing in arrears.

'The people down there in the black land behind the village, which I am anxious to reclaim, don't pay rent. They are broken men, broken sometimes by their own fault and laziness, sometimes by culpable imprudence, sometimes by stress of circumstances. When I settle a man there I build him a house, make him a present of a bit of land, give him tools, should he require them, and set him to work. He has the entire control of all he can produce. He improves my land, and can, if he is industrious, make a comfortable living. I won't have a pauper on my place: the very sight of a pauper sickens me.'

By the 1870s, however, such catastrophes as the potato famine had drawn the attention of the wider world to the recent history and present plight of the people of the Highlands and Islands. William Fraser and others began to attract unfavourable attention from parts of the press. In 1874 the *North British Daily Mail* in Glasgow described the situation in northern Skye as 'feudalism and tenant-at-willism, with the heavy rents that keep the people from ever getting out of difficulties'.

In 1877 heavy rain caused floods in north Skye, and a landslip 'which thundered down in terrible volume to Uig Bay' destroyed William Fraser's residence at Uig Lodge, as well as disinterring cadavers from the nearby graveyard and depositing them in what remained of Fraser's garden. The symbolism was irresistible to John Murdoch's *The Highlander*, which reported that 'The belief is common throughout the parish that the disaster is a judgement upon Captain Fraser . . .'

William Fraser sued *The Highlander* for damages to the tune of £1,000 in an attempt to put the magazine out of business. He was awarded £50 in damages and £35 in expenses, which was covered by Murdoch's friends and sympathisers. *The Highlander* survived, and William Fraser had made yet more enemies.

In the same year of 1877 Norman Stewart, a crofter and salmon fisherman from Valtos in the eastern, Staffin region of the Kilmuir estate, refused to pay a 60 per cent rent increase from £4.14s to £7.10s per annum for the use of half of an eight-acre croft. It is illuminative that Stewart was nicknamed 'Parnell' by his neighbours. The Irish Nationalist MP Charles Parnell's middle name was Stewart, which helped. Charles Stewart Parnell was clearly known in Skye in the late 1870s not only as a powerful advocate of Irish Home Rule, but also as a committed advocate of land reform and the first president of the Irish Land League. Whether or not Norman 'Parnell' Stewart was given to quoting or citing the Irishman in Kilmuir, or whether his neighbours simply recognised in their midst some village-Parnell, that with dauntless breast the little tyrant of his fields withstood, the nickname stuck.

Norman Stewart had already been jailed for a few days for taking unauthorised heather and rushes to thatch his crofthouse. In 1877 he was 44 years old and was married with four young children. The landowner's epitome of a troublemaker, 'Parnell' was nonetheless regarded with sufficient respect by his fellows in Valtos to be elected as their official spokesman to a Government Commission. His testament was only too typical. He and his people had too little land and were allowed to keep insufficient numbers of sheep and cattle – in Stewart's case he had two cows and 'seven or eight' sheep. Norman Stewart was specific about the amount of land and cattle needed to sustain a Kilmuir family for a year. They required 'from 15 to 20 acres of arable land . . . Ten cows, two horses and fifty sheep.' There was 'plenty' of land in the district to offer that to every man, and a reasonable annual rent of £10 to £12 would happily be paid in return.

Instead, the Valtos people 'are poorer than I can tell. It is hardly credible. When they go for a boll of meal from the dealer, the animal the dealer has to get for it must be marked before they can get the meal . . . It is a poor place that does not give a return . . . It is the rents [increases] that brought us first to poverty. We were in good circumstances until then . . . They are in want of clothes and in want of food.' There were families which had no bedclothes or blankets, said 'Parnell', and children with no shoes and stockings 'and cannot go to school for the want of them'.

Norman Stewart organised a deputation of crofters to go to Uig and protest to factor Alexander MacDonald about the latest rent increases, which were the third such imposition since William Fraser had bought Kilmuir estate, at a time when there was no inflation whatsoever and the value of the pound sterling was either steady or slightly increasing. In Uig, 'The factor asked us to try it for one year.' The crofters agreed. Another three years passed and the 'trial' of increased rental appeared to be both permanent and insupportable. A few offered to pay only the former, smaller rental, and some joined Norman Stewart in a rent strike.

By 1881 the Valtos rent strike involved 12 crofters and had spread to the nearby township of Ellishadder. Trouble was also brewing in the vicinity of the sheep farm at Monkstadt on the west coast of Kilmuir estate. In a fit of anger William Fraser told Alexander MacDonald to issue warnings of eviction to the 12 Valtos and Ellishadder men, making sure not to 'overlook Stewart of Valtos'. Some rental was then paid. At a peculiarly significant moment on 18 April 1881 the original Parnell, Charles Stewart Parnell, addressed a meeting in Glasgow which noted the eviction threats in Kilmuir and passed a motion pledging support for the 'struggle' of Highland crofters. Three weeks later in the same city the Federation of Celtic Societies also offered their backing specifically to the crofters of Valtos.

Alexander MacDonald in particular, being a Skyeman and a Gaelic speaker, was anxious not to fan too many flames and the factor recommended to Fraser that a swathe of rebates and actual rent reductions, diplomatically couched as compensation for bad weather, poor harvests and the reluctance of banks to offer loans to crofters, could usefully defuse the situation. William Fraser, whose position in the Inverness-shire Liberal Association was beginning to look anomalous, became suddenly receptive to such proposals. Following some unsatisfactory offers and rejections, in the summer of 1881 a 25 per cent rent rebate was offered to and accepted by every crofter on the Kilmuir estate – 'We got a slight reduction . . . £1 2s 6p,' said Norman 'Parnell' Stewart. It was by no means the end of the trouble in Kilmuir, but it was widely regarded there and in the wider world as a concession won by some militant crofters on behalf of the entire tenantry. As at Bernera in the west of Lewis seven years earlier, a crack was seen to have appeared in the battlements of landed interest. A domino effect was immediately apparent.

If Kilmuir was a smouldering muir-burn, a bush fire then erupted in Braes. The district of Braes was not a peninsula but an equally isolated string of crofting townships which ran along a narrow littoral between low hills and the Sound of Raasay down the east coast of central Skye.

Once again, the immediate cause of the conflagration was confiscated common grazings. The villages of Braes lay in the shadow of Ben Lee, an extensive, elevated stretch of rough pasture upon which they had until 1865 grazed their stock. Their landlord, Macdonald of Sleat, then let out Ben Lee to a sheep farm. In 1881 the sheep farm's lease was about to expire. 'We have particular cause for speaking in our own interest as regards the hill of Benlee which was taken from us,' said Samuel Nicolson of Balmeanach two years later. 'I can point out to the present day the sheilings which the women had in my grandfather's time on the hill, and we were looking upon it that we had full right of the grazing on Benlee.'

Samuel Nicolson's assertion was given unintentional support from a most unexpected quarter. In a clumsy attempt to assist his fellow clan chief by denigrating the actual value of Ben Lee, in 1883 MacLeod of MacLeod wrote to the Highland newspapers from London: 'Ben Lee was a Common, and as is well known, what is common to all is of little value to any.' Ben Lee was in fact capable of accommodating well over a thousand sheep, which were of considerable value to the crofters of Braes. As their rents had not been reduced following the privatisation of Ben Lee, and had actually increased in the following years, the crofters reasoned that they were under no obligation to pay for the hill's return as they had never stopped leasing it.

The Braes crofters petitioned Alexander MacDonald, who was by then factor for Lord Macdonald of Sleat as well as for William Fraser of Kilmuir, having assumed the former position in 1879 from Donald 'Tormore' MacDonald, to have Ben Lee returned to them in exchange for a fair rental. When their petition was rejected they followed the example recently set in Valtos and Ellishadder and announced a rent strike, while simultaneously driving some of their stock onto Ben Lee.

Ronald Archibald Bosville Macdonald, the 29–year-old 6th Baron Macdonald, and his factor Alexander MacDonald decided to act ruthlessly and promptly. They raised notices of eviction against seven men and three women (all three of whom were widows) who they considered to be the ringleaders of a troublesome faction in Braes. On 7 April 1882 Sheriff Officer Angus Martin, who had previously worked as a clerk for the factor Alexander MacDonald, his assistant Ewen Robertson and the estate ground officer Norman Beaton left Portree to deliver the notices. Two youngsters who had been put on sentry duty at the northern entrance to Braes promptly raised the alarm. Between 150 and 200 men and women – the total population of Braes was around 300 people – rushed to intercept the officers before they could reach the townships.

The following week the *Aberdeen Daily Free Press* reported: 'We have received the following narrative of the manner in which the summonses were burned [in Braes] on Friday last: – The people met the officer on the road, about a mile from the scene of his intended labours. They were clamorous and angry, of course. He told them his mission, and that he would give them the summonses on the spot if they liked. They said, "Thoir dhuinn iad," (Give them to us) and he did so.

'The officer was then asked to light a fire. He did so; and a fish liver being placed upon it, that oily material was soon in a blaze. The officer was then peremptorily ordered to consign the summonses to the flames, which he did! The summonses were of course straightway consumed to ashes. The interchange of compliments between the officers of the law and the people were, as might be expected, of a fiery character.

'The chief officer [Angus Martin] was graciously and considerately informed that his conduct – as he had only acted in the performance of a public official duty – was excusable; but with his assistant, or concurrent [Ewen Robertson], it was different.

He was there for pay, and he would not go home without it. Certain domestic utensils, fully charged, were suddenly brought on the scene, and their contents were showered on the unlucky assistant, who immediately disappeared, followed by a howling crowd of boys.'

Whatever offences may or may not have been committed earlier, the law was unequivocally broken in Braes on 7 April. A sheriff officer had been deforced and his assistant had been assaulted. It was time for William Ivory to intervene.

The 56–year-old William Ivory was yet another son of a distinguished Edinburgh family. His father, Lord James Ivory, had been solicitor-general for Scotland and a High Court judge. His brother Francis became a legislator in Australia. William himself qualified as an advocate before becoming, in 1862, the sheriff of Inverness-shire, Elgin and Nairn. Sheriff William Ivory would hold that position until the year 1900 while continuing to live mostly at his large family household in Edinburgh. While on business in the north he sometimes based himself in a comfortable pied-a-terre at Auchindoun in the Nairnshire countryside, halfway between Inverness and Aberdeen. Auchindoun was not very far from the birthplace of William Fraser of Kilmuir or from the Nairnshire holdings of Donald 'Tormore' MacDonald. It was nonetheless both culturally and geographically a long way from the island of Skye.

His social, familial and professional background therefore put William Ivory, the principal law officer in Inverness-shire, firmly on one side of the land question. He would do nothing in the 1880s to confound his friends and associates.

Upon receiving news of the affray at Braes on 7 April, Ivory sprang into action. Frustrated by the fact that there were only 44 police officers in the whole of Inverness-shire, which given their other everyday duties was an insufficient number for a serious punitive expedition, he appealed through his police committee for assistance from the City of Glasgow Police, which employed well over 1,000 officers. Men in uniform were sent north, and in the early morning of 19 April 1882, 'in weather that for sheer brutal ferocity had not been experienced in Skye for a very long time', a majestic procession of 40 Glaswegian policemen (at least a few of whom, given the composition at the time of the City of Glasgow Police, were likely to have been exiled Highlanders), ten from the Inverness-shire mainland, a handful of their colleagues from Skye, the Portree sheriff officer, the two procurators fiscal from Inverness and Skye, Sheriff William Ivory, the 39–year-old Skye Sheriff-Substitute Peter Speirs and several journalists set forth from Portree to march the eight miles into Braes to arrest the men who had threatened and deforced Sheriff Officer Angus Martin 12 days earlier.

One of those journalists, Alexander Gow of the *Dundee Advertiser*, reported: 'Arrived at the boundary of Balmeanach, we found a collection of men, women, and children, numbering well on to 100. They cheered as we mounted the knoll, and the women saluted the policemen with volleys of sarcasm about their voyage from Glasgow.

'A halt was then called, and a parley ensued between the local inspector and what appeared to be the leader of the townships. What is passing between the two it is difficult for an outsider to understand, and while the conversation is in progress it is worth while to look about. At the base of the steep cliff on which we stood, and extending to the seashore, lay the hamlet of Balmeanach. There might be about a score of houses dotted over this plain. From each of these the owners were running hillward with all speed. It was evident they had been taken by surprise. Men, women, and children rushed forward, in all stages of attire, most of the females with their hair down and streaming loosely in the breeze. Every soul carried a weapon of some kind or another, but in most cases these were laid down when the detachment was approached.

'While we were watching the crowds scrambling up the declivity, scores of persons had gathered from other districts, and they now completely surrounded the procession. The confusion that prevailed baffles description. The women, with infuriated looks and bedraggled dress – for it was still raining heavily – were shouting at the pitch of their voices, uttering the most fearful imprecations, hurling forth the most terrible vows of vengeance against the enemy . . .

'The authorities proceeded at once to perform their disagreeable task, and in the course of twenty minutes the five suspected persons were apprehended. A scene utterly indescribable followed. The women, with the most violent gestures and imprecations, declared that the police should be attacked. Stones began to be thrown, and so serious an aspect did matters assume that the police drew their batons and charged. This was the signal for a general attack. Huge boulders darkened the horizon as they sped from the hands of infuriated men and women. Large sticks and flails were brandished and brought down with crushing force upon the police – the poor prisoners coming in for their share of the blows. One difficult point had to be captured, and as the expedition approached this dangerous position, it was seen to be strongly occupied with men and women, armed with stones and boulders.

'A halt was called and the situation discussed. Finally it was agreed to attempt to force a way through a narrow gully. By this time a crowd had gathered in the rear of the party. A rush was made for the pass, and from the heights a fearful fusilade of stones descended. The advance was checked. The party could neither advance nor recede. For two minutes the expedition stood exposed to the merciless shower of missiles. Many were struck, and a number more or less injured. The situation was highly dangerous.

'Raising a yell that might have been heard at a distance of two miles, the crofters, maddened by the apprehension of some of the oldest men in the township, rushed on the police, each person armed with huge stones, which, on approaching near enough, they discharged with a vigour that nothing could resist. The women were by far the most troublesome assailants.

Thinking apparently that the constables would offer them no resistance, they approached to within a few yards' distance, and poured a fearful volley into the compact mass.

'The police charged, but the crowd gave way scarcely a yard. Returning again, Captain Donald gave orders to drive back the howling mob, at the same time advising the Sheriffs and the constables in charge of the prisoners to move rapidly forward. This second charge was more effective, as the attacking force was driven back about a hundred yards. The isolated constables now, however, found their position very dangerous. The crofters rallied and hemmed them in, and a rush had to be made to catch up the main body in safety. At this point several members of the constabulary received serious buffetings, and had they not regained their comrades, some of their number would in all probability have been mortally wounded. Meanwhile the crowd increased in strength . . .

'Hundreds of determined looking persons could be observed converging on the procession, and matters began to assume a serious aspect. With great oaths, the men demanded where were the Peinichorrain men. This township was the most distant, and the men had not yet had time to come up. But they were coming. Cheers and yells were raised. "The rock! The rock!" suddenly shouted some one. "The rock! The rock!" was taken up, and roared out from a hundred throats. The strength of the position was realised by the crofters; so also it was by the constables. The latter were ordered to run at the double. The people saw the move, and the screaming and yelling became fiercer than ever. The detachment reached the opening of the gulley. Would they manage to run through? Yes! No! On went the blue coats, but their progress was soon checked. It was simply insane to attempt the passage.

'Stones were coming down like hail, while huge boulders where hurled down before which nothing could stand. These bounded over the road and descended the precipice with a noise like thunder. An order was given to dislodge a number of the most determined assailants, but the attempt proved futile. They could not be dislodged. Here and there a constable might be seen actually bending under the pressure of a well-directed boulder, losing his footing, and rolling down the hill, followed by scores of missiles.

'This state of matters could not continue. The chief officials were securing their share of attention. Captain Donald is hit in the knee with a stone as large as a matured turnip. A rush must be made for the pass, or there seems a possibility that Sheriff Ivory himself will be deforced. Once more the order was given to double. On, on, the procession went – Sheriffs and Fiscals forgetting their dignity, and taking to their heels. The scene was the most exciting that either the spectators or those who passed through the fire ever experienced, or are likely ever to see again. By keeping up the rush, the party got through the defile, and emerged triumphantly on the Portree side, not however, without severe injuries. If the south end township [of Peinchorran] had turned out, the pass would, I believe, never have been forced, and some would in all probability have lost their lives.

'The crofters seemed to have become more infuriated by the loss of their position, and rushing along the shoulder of the hill prepared to attack once more. This was the final struggle. In other attacks the police used truncheons freely. But at this point they retaliated with both truncheons and stones. The consequences were very serious indeed. Scores of bloody faces could be seen on the slope of the hill. One woman, named Mary Nicolson, was fearfully cut in the head, and fainted on the road. When she was found, blood was pouring down her neck and ears. Another woman, Mrs. Finlayson, was badly gashed on the cheek with some missile. Mrs. Nicolson, whose husband, James Nicolson, was one of the prisoners, had her head badly laid open, but whether with a truncheon or stone is not known.

'Another woman, well advanced in years, was hustled in the scrimmage on the hill, and, losing her balance, rolled down a considerable distance, her example being followed by a stout policeman, the two ultimately coming into violent collision. The poor old person was badly bruised, and turned sick and faint. Of the men a considerable number sustained severe bruises, but so far as I could ascertain none of them were disabled. About a dozen of the police were injured more or less seriously. One of the Glasgow men had his nose almost cut through with a stone, and was terribly gashed about the brow. Captain Donald, as already stated, was struck on the knee, and his leg swelled up badly after the return to Portree. Neither the Sheriffs nor the Fiscals were injured, but it is understood that they all received hits in the encounter on the hill.

'After the serious scrimmage at Gedintailler, no further demonstrations of hostility were made, and the procession went on, without further adventure, to Portree. Rain fell without intermission during the entire journey out and home, and all arrived at their destination completely exhausted. On arrival in town the police were loudly hooted and hissed as they passed through the square to the jail, and subsequently when they marched from the Court-house to the Royal Hotel. The prisoners were lodged in the prison. Their names are: – Alexander Finlayson, aged between 60 and 70 years; Malcolm Finlayson, a son of the above, and living in the same house (the latter is married); Peter Macdonald has a wife and eight of a family; Donald Nicolson, 66 years of age, and is married; and James Nicolson, whose wife was one of the women seriously injured.'

This incident, which quickly became known as the Battle of the Braes, was more than a mere skirmish. It was a committed and extremely violent attempt by almost an entire civilian community to defy and defeat representatives of the law of the land in the legitimate prosecution of their duties. The absence of serious injury or even death at Braes on 19 April 1882 was purely fortuitous. The severity of the battle was greater than that of any industrial dispute of the time. It came very close to being a Highland Peterloo. What was more, it was clear that the rebellious small community enjoyed widespread support in

the rest of Skye, throughout the Highlands and Islands, and
in substantial urban pockets of the United Kingdom. A Braes
Defence Committee was quickly established in Glasgow. When
the five prisoners were eventually granted bail from Inverness
Prison at £20 per head, a collection of Highland businessmen
queued up to offer their financial support and the £100 total
bail bond was guaranteed by Mr John Macdonald, merchant,
Exchange; Dean of Guild Alexander Mackenzie; Councillor
Duncan Macdonald; Councillor W.G. Stuart; Mr William
Gunn, Castle Street; Mr T.B. Snowie, gunmaker; Mr Donald
Campbell, draper; and Mr Duncan MacBeath of Duncraig
Street. 'By this time,' reported Alexander Gow, 'the sympathy
with the prisoners among the outside public, not merely in the
Highlands but in the large cities of the south, had extended
through all classes of society.'

All five of the Braes men were found guilty of assault at Inverness
Sheriff Court. A cheque for the full amount of their fines was
promptly handed over by their supporters. 'The prisoners, who
had been confined between two policemen throughout the day,
were then liberated. As they emerged from the Castle, they were
met by a large crowd, who greeted them with cheers and calls for
a speech. They, however, were allowed to proceed to their hotel
without any further demonstration. The men and the witnesses
were lodged, and provided with a liberal supply of all the creature
comforts, in the Glenalbyn Hotel, where they were visited by
many of those in Inverness who sympathised with their position.
Next morning they left by train and steamer for Portree, their
fares having been paid, and provision made for anything they
might require on the journey. On their arrival the same evening in
the Capital of Skye they were met by their friends and the people
of Portree, who greeted them with great enthusiasm, and many of
whom convoyed them the greater part of their way to the Braes.'
Before the end of the year Lord Macdonald and his agents had
concluded that, as 'the law is no longer respected in Skye', they
would return Ben Lee to the Braes crofters for an annual rent of

£74.15s. It was by no means the end of the matter – collecting that £74 would prove to be difficult – but the people of the district could claim a victory.

Shortly before the verdict on the five Braes men was delivered, the National Land League of Great Britain thought it timeous to send John Murdoch and the Irish–Glaswegian Edward McHugh to Skye. Unlike Murdoch, McHugh was not a fluent speaker of Scottish Gaelic. His mission was ill-conceived in other ways. The National Land League of Great Britain was, as its name suggests, anxious to knit together different expressions of radical theory and action from across the whole of the United Kingdom. Edward McHugh therefore took with him, into the heart of the Gaidhealtachd, a suitcase of English-language pamphlets such as the 'Report of the Durham Miners' delegates on the state of Ireland; Democratic Federation Report; Cleveland Miners' Report; "Nationalisation of the Land", by Dr G.B. Clark, "The Land for the People", by John Ferguson, "The Irish Land Question: what it involves and how it alone can be settled", by Henry George; and Sexton's splendid speech, "The Land League Vindicated" . . .'

A day or two before John Murdoch and Edward McHugh arrived in Skye they were preceded by a leaflet in both Gaelic and English, titled 'Address to the People' and authored by Sheriff-Substitute Alexander Nicolson of the Stewartry of Kirkcudbright. Although he was serving in the far south-west of Scotland, Alexander Nicolson was the most celebrated Skyeman of his time. Nicolson was actually a native of Glendale, having been born at Husabost in 1827 when his father owned that part of the district which would later be taken over by Dr Nicol Martin. Alexander Nicolson was a pioneering climber – the peak Sgurr Alasdair in the Cuillins was named for him – a prolific writer about Skye and the Highlands in general, and a proselytiser for the Gaelic language.

He was also, as his pamphlet made clear, true to his origins in the Highland landholding classes.

'A mhuinntir mo cridhe! . . .' read Nicolson's 'Address to
the People', 'People of my Heart, – What dreadful news is this
that has come to us about you! Little did I think I should ever
hear of the like coming from the island I love, particularly from
Glendale, the country of my youth, and the Braes of Portree,
the country of my ancestors, whose nature it was to be peaceable people, I am very sorrowful today. Small is my delight in
thinking of the island that I have so often praised. We were
sorrowful to hear of your great losses at the beginning of winter;
but this news is far more grievous.

'Many a man, I am sure, in places far away will feel the same.
I was lately in Edinburgh giving a short account, with much
satisfaction, of the Highlanders, and I said, "though they have
suffered much, and some of them suffer still, they are very
different from the miserable Irish. As the old saying has it,
'O'Brien was very different from the Gael.'

'"The Highlander is manly, spirited, but he is sensible, devout,
quiet, honest, courteous. He will not give bad language in return for
bad usage. He will not refuse to pay the rent, though it be difficult
for him. He does not seek the land for himself; he seeks only justice,
and to be allowed to live in the place where he was born."

'But now, alas, Skyemen are imitating the Irish, and making
themselves objects of derision and dread. My dear friends, don't
think it so you will get justice. Nothing will come of it but
trouble and shame. And now it has come with a vengeance!

'My heart is sore to think of it. I heard with disgust that I was
mentioned myself in Skye as one of those who were stirring up
the people to mischief, and telling them that the land belonged
to themselves. I said nothing of the kind. I am not so ignorant
or so mad as to use such language.

'As St Paul said, "Oh foolish Galatians, who hath bewitched
you?" I beseech you do not forget that excellent old saying:
Follow close the fame of your fathers. Their fame ever was to
be trustworthy, orderly, honourable, obedient to the law. If
you have any real causes of complaint, there is no fear but you

will get justice: but it is not by violence and uproar, and high-handedness that you will get it.

'"He that breaks the law breaks his own head." In the name of everything that is good and praiseworthy, bring no shame on our name, and sorrow to all our true friends, whether Highland or Lowland.

'Finally, brethren, whatsoever things are true, whatsoever things are honest, whatsoever things are just, whatsoever things are pure, whatsoever things are of good report: if there be any virtue, and if there be any praise, think on these things.

'From your faithful friend and fellow-countryman, Alexander Nicolson, who was born in Husabost, now residing in Kirkcudbright.'

Murdoch and McHugh encountered Nicolson's address in Skye. John Murdoch later irritably recorded that, 'I met two clergymen in the town of Portree, one of them with a bundle of copies of a silly leaflet in Gaelic which a sheriff in another part of Scotland printed to act as a wet-sheet on the minds of the people. . . "Oh, we sympathise with the people," the younger of the two said, while the other seemed ashamed of the bundle of twaddle which he had been asked to circulate.'

Edward McHugh was also hampered by epochal events elsewhere. Ten days after he and Murdoch landed in Portree on 26 April 1882, Irish republicans stabbed to death in Dublin's Phoenix Park Lord Frederick Cavendish, the new Chief Secretary for Ireland, and his senior civil servant, Thomas Henry Burke. The Irish nationalist parliamentary leader Charles Stewart Parnell condemned the murders but press and public reaction throughout England, Wales and Scotland was unappeasable. Opponents of everything and anything Irish, including land reform, the 'Erse' language in all of its forms and, most crucially, Home Rule, raised havoc. The taint cannot but have attached itself to Edward McHugh in Skye.

Moreover, although his message was a lay matter, McHugh found himself as a radical Roman Catholic in a staunchly

Presbyterian island whose Free Church and Church of Scotland ministers loudly and frequently condemned Popery to their congregations. The chief sergeant of police in Portree, Malcolm MacDonald, wrote to tell Sheriff William Ivory that McHugh's 'Roman Catholicism was very much against him.' John Murdoch was of course aware of that tension, but he clung to the hope that shared political aspirations would bridge the confessional chasm – as, to some extent, they did. But ultimately, McHugh was promoting the Land League's solution of nationalisation to a people who were mostly not convinced that such a dramatic reversal of the old order was either necessary or desirable.

The two men were nonetheless welcomed courteously in the crofting townships of Skye. McHugh made no attempt to enter the island surreptitiously or to deny either his presence or his purpose. His hosts were more cautious. McHugh's talks were advertised only by word of mouth, and for years afterwards few Skye men or women – who faced summary eviction for requesting the return of hill pasture, let alone for harbouring seditious Irishmen – would admit to having heard of, let alone met or listened to, Edward McHugh in the May and June of 1882.

Local landholding interests, which were anxious to deflect attention away from their own incitements to violence in Skye and onto agents provocateurs, were less shy. Alexander Smith's brother-in-law, Alex MacDonald of Ord, who inherited his father's 5,000–acre tack but not the old man's paternal attitude towards his tenants (young Ord described his farm as being surrounded on one side by the sea and 'unfortunately' on the other three sides by crofters), would say in 1883 that the 'discontent in Skye ... began, so far as my knowledge goes, in the north end of the island by two gentlemen – the one an Irishman named McHugh, and the other named Murdoch – who came among the people to tell them of their rights; and I suppose, the seasons having been bad, and many other causes of that kind, made them think it was a good time to make their demonstrations. That is my opinion.'

Young Ord's friend and neighbour, Donald 'Tormore' MacDonald, supported the thesis. 'I have not the slightest hesitation,' said Tormore, 'in saying that the literature that was distributed among the people of this country was the first mover in this unfortunate rebellion; and, without naming many, I will name the principal paper that came here, and that was the famous but fortunately now defunct *Highlander*. The editor of the *Highlander*, I believe, is still alive and going about. I saw in one of the papers that he was to be down here educating the people in rebellion. I have not seen him, but I am not sorry he is not here. Well, I will pass him over, – he is not worth powder; and I will come to No. 2, – Mr McHugh, the secretary of the Irish Land Reform Association in Glasgow.'

Aside from anything else, the two MacDonalds' chronology was wildly astray. 'The discontent in Skye' had been manifest in Kilmuir, Braes, Glendale and elsewhere long before Edward McHugh disembarked at Portree seven days after the Battle of the Braes, and had been caused by internal disputes rather than outside agitators. The clerk of the court in Portree, Dugald Maclachlan, who significantly was born into the native bourgeoisie but had arrived in Skye as a teenager from the Argyllshire island of Mull, would state in public that the 'expression of discontent and rebellion . . . is certainly not attributable to Irish agitators'.

Just one elderly Skye crofter confessed to giving beds to McHugh and Murdoch in the early summer of 1882. The 64–year-old John Campbell of Hamara in Glendale told a Government inquiry in the following year, 'I know that Tormore was displeased with me; and I heard it said, and I am not going to deny it, that I gave hospitality to two individuals who were going about among the people, and Tormore threatened that he would do for me because of that.

'I said to him,' continued Campbell, 'that I never denied hospitality to any one so long as he would behave himself in my house. He told me I was only keeping a bad house, giving lodgement to Irishmen and to blackguards, and he ran down both myself and my house and my family. He said I would not give him hospitality, and I told him I would, and that I was kinder than that towards his business and his servants ever since he came into my neighbourhood.'

Intrigued by this rare admission, the chairman of the inquiry asked John Campbell to expound – 'You said you kept two strangers in your house? What were the names of the strangers?'

'M'Hugh, an Irishman,' said Campbell, 'and Mr Murdoch was the other.'

'Was Murdoch an Irishman or a Scotchman?'

'He was a Highlander; he was formerly editor of the *Highlander* newspaper.'

'Did they both stay with you for some time?'

'Yes.'

'How long did they stay?'

'They came on the Saturday to the Glen and reached Meiloveg, and they were late, and when they returned they came to my house, and they left on Monday.'

'They only stayed from Saturday till Monday?'

'Yes.'

'How did they employ the Sabbath?'

'Murdoch went to church. He came to hear the sermon here. The other man could not understand Gaelic, and did not go.'

'What business brought McHugh here?'

'To enlighten the people on something, but I would not understand what he was saying.'

'What language did he speak?'

'English.'

'Did he hold a public meeting?'

'Not many gathered to hear him, at any rate.'

'What did he tell the people?'

'He was telling the public to plead for good justice, and to get more land, and advising them that they were not to break the law in any way.'

'And when he went away, where did he go to?'

'I think it was to Uist.'

'He only remained here from Saturday till Monday?'

'Yes, that is all.'

'Did he ever come back again?'

'Yes, and he gave me a call when he returned.'

'How long did he stay the second time?'

'He came about six o'clock at night, and left in the morning.'

'Were there ever any other Irish gentlemen came here?'

'No, no other.'

'Did he visit any other place about here?'

'I don't know what places the man visited.'

'Do you know what part of Ireland he came from?'

'No, nothing about it.'

'He could not speak Gaelic?'

'No.'

'Did he come from Glasgow?'

'He was saying it was from Glasgow he came to this place.'

Before leaving Skye, John Murdoch paid a visit to his old adversary, Donald 'Tormore' MacDonald at Hamara Lodge, the factor's house in Glendale. 'I said to Mr Macdonald,' Murdoch would later report, 'It is so difficult to arrive at the truth in regard to what has been going on in these quarters that I have come to inquire on the spot.'

'"Yes," said he, "and you have come to do more mischief . . ."

'"Stop," I said, "you have known me for some years now, did you ever know me even to attempt to do mischief?"

'"Well, no," he said at once . . .

'Calming down, he entered into conversation with me on the troubles with which he was beset. Having dilated on the great change for the worse, which had come over the people, he took down a revolver from the chimney piece, saying, "So bad have the people become that I am obliged to carry that with me."'

In truth, by the spring of 1882 Donald 'Tormore' MacDonald had good reason to carry a firearm in Glendale.

SIX

Who will Take the Crofters?

SIR JOHN MACPHERSON MACLEOD, the owner of the Glendale estate, died in London in 1881. Before his death he had sold back the St Kilda islands to the MacLeods of Dunvegan, another generation of which line was by the 1870s prospering in London.

Glendale was, however, put into a trust for the childless Sir John's nephew, a 23–year-old keen ornithologist and future Church of Scotland minister named Hugh Alexander Macpherson. Reverend Macpherson's fellow trustees of Glendale estate were two other relatives, a Lowland sheriff named Norman Macpherson and his brother William, who was an advocate. Those three men initially retained the services of Donald 'Tormore' MacDonald as factor.

On Whitsunday, 15 May 1882, the lease of Waterstein farm was due to expire. Old, tired and exasperated by the local crofters' disregard for his position and legal rights, Dr Nicol Martin had made it clear that he did not wish to renew his lease. The crofters, he would lament, 'are getting indolent and lazy besides. Look at this winter; they did nothing but go about with fires on every hill, and playing sentinels to watch for fear of sheriff's officers coming with warnings to take their cattle for rent. They went about with pitch-forks and scythes and poles pointed with iron or steel, and it was a mercy no one would serve the processes upon them, or they would have murdered him sure enough. You cannot get a sheriff's officer now to serve a process on any tenant in Skye . . . migrate them; [let them] go where they like. I don't see who would take them . . .'

The crofters of Milovaig in particular had no intention of going anywhere other than to Waterstein. Early in 1882 – long before the Battle of the Braes at the other side of Skye – they held meetings to discuss this and other ambitions. The crofters would consistently deny that such meetings constituted the formation of such an overtly political body as a local land league. The term was not used by them at the time. 'We the tenants on the estate of Glendale,' read a notice in Glendale post office, 'do hereby warn each other to meet at Glendale Church on the 7th day of February, on or about one p.m. of 1882, for the purpose of stating our respective grievances publicly in order to communicate them to our superiors, when the ground officer is requested to attend.'

'I don't think we made any alliance – no distinct binding of ourselves individually,' said John MacPherson of Lower Milovaig later. 'All the alliance we made between ourselves was that we wanted to get Waterstein to help us, as we were poor, and as Dr Martin who had the place gave it up, and that we had as much right as anybody else to get it, as we were as much in need of it. We were more needy than those who had five or six tacks already, seeing that they had only one mouth and two hands like ourselves, and seeing that we were quite willing to give as much rent as they could give.'

MacPherson was being economical with the truth. A local land league was formed in Glendale in 1882. 'As I heard the anecdotal history from my grandfather,' said Allan Campbell, 'and then from Neil MacLean of Milovaig in 1982 there seemed absolutely no doubt that a Glendale Land League had been established at the February meeting of 1882. This was further reinforced in an interview which I discovered between the former BBC producer James Ross and his father Norman Ross. Norman was about 12 years old in 1882 and gave an eye-witness account of some of the events. My grandfather always referred to the 1880s as "àm an Land League", "the Land League time".

'There is an interview in the BBC's Gaelic archive between Hugh MacPhee and a retired school teacher, originally from Borrodale, which was recorded in the late 1930s or 1940s. The schoolteacher told how he was a schoolboy in his early teens at the time of the Land League and how – because he was literate in English – he wrote letters for the Land League committee. He specifically mentioned writing to John Murdoch and Edward McHugh, as well as to the Prime Minister of the day.'

The Glendale crofters and Land Leaguers insisted upon, and achieved to a remarkable extent in a district of almost 2,000 people, the rough discipline of a revolutionary cell. In March 1882 further notices in the post office warned of a rent strike: 'Any one of the tenants at Skinidin who will pay the rent, not only that his House and Property will be destroyed, but his life will be taken away or anyone who will begin backsliding. Not to be removed.' And: 'Notice is hereby given by the Milovaig and Borrodale Alliance that Doctor Martin must clear Waterstein of his stock at Whitsunday punctually, if not, they will be driven off with full force.'

'I am extremely sorry,' commented their factor, Donald 'Tormore' MacDonald, 'to find that the people denied the existence of a land league, and a knowledge of the notices which were being put up. I can speak personally as to both, having seen some of the notices, and I believe they are still to be found. As to their being bound by a league, there is plenty evidence to prove that they said and believed they were under such a bond, for they repeatedly said to me that they were so, and sworn to stand by each other against all law and against all force till their demands were complied with.'

In the short term, whether Glendale contained a land league by name or merely by approximation, the crofters of the Milovaig neighbourhood devoted themselves to winning

Waterstein. Initially they did this in the most legitimate manner possible – they put in a bid for the lease.

Given the amount of time and ink which had been devoted to urging Highland crofters to take full financial responsibility for their own land and affairs, that seemed to be the ideal and obvious solution for all parties. And initially, it appeared to be all but signed and delivered. In full anticipation of regaining the land, as well as with an intention of pressing the issue, the crofters began to restock Waterstein with their own cattle and sheep.

'When we heard that Waterstein was vacant,' said John MacPherson, 'we sent a letter to our factor; and we told him how great our need was of the hill, and how many families and souls there were between the two townships, and that we were thinking he would see it proper to let us have the hill, when we were willing to pay the rent for it. He replied to us telling us that our landlord was coming to the place, and that he himself was coming to Colbost; and our landlord sent us word that the factor was coming to Colbost, and he asked us to meet the factor there. We told him what we were wanting, and he told us that he himself had taken Waterstein, but that he would give it up for our sakes . . .'

Tormore asked the Milovaig and Borrodale crofters 'what rent we would give for it'.

'We said that although we should make an offer somebody else might give a higher offer, and he told us that there was nobody to give a higher offer but himself, and that he would not do it; and that we were to write him as to how we proposed to take it, and that he would write to the trustees on our behalf.

'We wrote and told him that we would give the same rent that Dr Martin was paying for it, and we also sent a petition to the trustees saying to them that we would leave it to their own consciences whether it would be more proper to give the place to us, while we were willing to pay the rent for it, and our arrears, or to give it to Tormore, who had already Dibidale,

Ollisdale, Lowergill, Ramasaig, Hamara, Ostaig, Park of Nairn, and Craggie, and who, as I have already said, had only one mouth and two hands and one body like ourselves.'

Tormore had promised the crofters Waterstein, said John MacPherson, 'in presence of two hundred witnesses. He then sent us word saying that the trustees were coming to see us, and that they would put matters right with us. The trustees did come, in May [1882], and the weather was bad the night they came, but in spite of that there was a bonfire on every hilL

'When they were a week in the place we went to them, and they gave us no satisfaction, but told us to have patience. We told them that our forefathers had died in good patience, and that we ourselves had been waiting in patience till now, and that we could not wait any longer, – that they never got anything by their patience, but constantly getting worse.

'The trustees never said to us that we would not get the hill; but the first man who out-and-out refused was Tormore, the man who had promised it to us . . . Tormore did say to us that we would not get the hill, and we said to him that as he had promised us the hill before, we would retain possession of it until the trustees would deprive us of it.'

Shortly after Whitsunday 1882, Tormore handed in his resignation as factor to the trustees of the Glendale estate. He then 'went that day to Waterstein, and he began to clear off what sheep and cattle were on the hill – for there were sheep and cattle on the hill belonging to other townships as well as to ourselves – and he began to clear them off the hill on to our holdings. We said to him that we would not allow him to do such things, and he said in presence of all these people that he would bid good-bye to us, and that he would never see us again. He had his own stock upon the hill . . .'

Tormore never denied any of those assertions. Indeed, he confirmed them – 'I intimated . . . to the crofters that if they could satisfy the trustees that they could manage to stock and pay rent for Waterstein, or any part of the farm, that my agreement would not stand in the way of such an arrangement being carried out.' He contented himself with offering an explanation for the double-cross, which was that the crofters of Milovaig and Borrodale, who were on rent-strike, were not paying their own croft rents let alone the £140 a year demanded for Waterstein, ignoring the facts that the crofters offered their own 'stock on the ground' as security for the rent, and that they also had a guarantee of the Waterstein rent from a sympathetic 'gentleman . . . if we had got the place'. Having been anchored in poverty, Tormore considered that they were clearly unfit to elevate themselves.

Donald 'Tormore' MacDonald reported that he drove 'six hundred or seven hundred or eight hundred sheep of mine . . . from my farm in Nairnshire, with a view to stock [Waterstein], if the people would not interfere.'

The people did interfere, as he had suspected they would. 'The people would not allow the sheep on – at least prevented them going on part of the ground – and therefore the trustees could not implement their bargain with me, and I simply walked out of it . . .'

Even then, with Waterstein once again untenanted, the trustees refused to take the obvious conciliatory option of offering the lease of the farm to a combination of crofters for a trial period of time. The crofters thought that vested interests in Skye were responsible for turning the estate trustees against them – 'we were hearing that the trustees were gentlemen, and before they left Edinburgh they were saying they were going to come and see the place, but when they came to Skye, and went to visit gentlemen's houses in Skye they were in a different mind.'

A new factor, the 59–year-old John Robertson, was quickly appointed and directed to clear up the mess. John Robertson was a monoglot English speaker from Perthshire who, despite having lived in rural Ireland before settling in Grishornish 13 years earlier and becoming the tacksman of 16,000 acres of north-west Skye, employing 40 people there, had made no attempt to familiarise himself with the Gaelic language.

In a brusque and businesslike manner, John Robertson bought Tormore's Nairnshire sheep on behalf of his trustees and employed shepherds to care for them at Waterstein. He cleared what few of the crofters' animals remained, including some which Tormore had permitted to graze at Ramasaig, to the south of Waterstein. In the confusion, many sheep which were either unclaimed or owned by the estate were driven off Waterstein and actually grazed on the Milovaig crofters' sparse land for three months. In a clumsy attempt to defuse the situation, Robertson then offered the Milovaig crofters 'a piece of Waterstein for us which was next to our march, and which piece would not be worth much to the tacksman of Waterstein . . . we showed him before we parted that this piece which he was for adding to our holdings would not enable each of us to keep more than a sheep.'

It was akin to sowing the wind. The crofters of Glendale watched with anger and dismay, and pointed out that at least they had been able to discuss matters in their common tongue with Donald 'Tormore' MacDonald.

The whirlwind was quickly reaped. They continued to confirm their rent strike – 'they said that they would never pay a penny to the factor – that they would not pay to Mr Robertson especially . . . He is not a suitable factor for us, for he does not speak our language, and many of us cannot speak English.'

Like the people of Braes the people of Glendale did not really need leaders, any more than they had required the assistance of outside agitators. The communal nature of their daily lives – the work at the peats, at fishing, at gathering and shearing – had taught them since childhood to act together, to put aside petty individual differences in the interests of an essential common cause. But in this hour of bitter humiliation John MacPherson of Lower Milovaig stepped forward like some Old Testament prophet to articulate their case. 'It is as a speaker that John Macpherson is seen at his best,' said one reporter from outside Skye. 'When thundering forth his denunciations of the oppressor and the tyrant to an enthusiastic audience of his own countrymen, at one moment rousing them to the highest pitch with some faithfully-drawn picture of the wrongs suffered by the people, at another causing roars of merriment by some apt simile or well-aimed hit – it is then that one can fully realise and appreciate the power which Macpherson possesses over the minds and feelings of his fellow-Highlanders . . .'

There was no shortage of strong characters in any crofting community in the second half of the 19th century. MacPherson was assisted by such people as the Glendale sub-postmaster, Peter MacKinnon. In 1882 MacKinnon was 54 years old and living with his wife and seven children on a croft at Lephin in central Glendale. A native of Borrodale, south of Milovaig, he had joined the Royal Navy and fought in the Crimean War before being invalided out through injuries in 1860. MacKinnon returned to Glendale with a pension and a 'few hundred pounds of money at my command of my hard earnings'.

He was given permission by John Macpherson MacLeod to open a general store, which also became the Glendale post office, which under his management became in due course a clearing centre and meeting place for the rebellious people of the district. MacKinnon had long since fallen out with Donald 'Tormore' MacDonald, and by the early 1880s was able to boast of having received 'three summonses of removal within the last twenty years, without any reasonable cause, except imaginary and unfair accusations of the following natures: – 1. For claiming fair play and protection as a British subject; 2. For my being reading newspapers, thereby causing the enlightenment of my fellow-mortals; 3. Writing for poor people for admission of obtaining charity, &c.; 4. For speaking openly as shareholder of public opinion, as regarding voting for suitable members for Parliament and school boards, &c, for passing any remarks upon either Conservatism and Liberalisms; 5. Claiming good rules between factors and tenants, so as to have fair understanding between industrious honest crofters and honourable just landlords – until brought so very low as common degraded thief placed abaft the mizzen-mast, after undergoing punishment of the seven bell cat-of-nine-tails, but living in hopes of obtaining the usual quantity of sweet oil for soothing my scratches at the hour of sunset, so as to enable me drawing my pound and pint at five bells in the morning.'

Peter MacKinnon attested that 'the Meiloveg crofters could hardly bear the yoke placed upon their necks by the interdict of Tormore, to which the Supreme Court had given consent, in preventing landing or even standing upon any part of the lands between the point of Dibidal and Lower Meiloveg, the distance of about twelve miles, or taking out any licences or exemption paper for dogs, and from handling drift timber, under pain of their being reported by shepherds and herds. Under those circumstances of extreme depression, it appears that matters changed otherwise, when almost all the tenantry of the estate and of Dr Martin preferred hoisting a flag of independence against local rulers, at the same time unfurling their flag of distress for observation of the British Parliament.'

There was Alexander Ross, a 47–year-old from Fasach, who spoke indignantly of some of the hostile press coverage of the disruptions in Skye – 'We are hearing such reports even down from London. They are imputing to us in London, that we are a lawless people, and I will give you one case of the law which is in force here. Two steamers came to this parish for the past two years, and the place is very straitened with poverty, and want, and you may know that when the steamers are coming twice a week they are bringing plenty to eat, but there is no store-house in the place. The goods have to be placed on the shore in tarpaulins, and I never heard of a penny-worth being stolen of these goods during that time. There has been a policeman sent among us about a year ago, and he has not had a case yet except about one old teapot which he took from a tinker. The tinker's horse had eaten some corn belonging to a woman, and the policeman went for the woman to get him to pay for the damage.'

There was 53–year-old Peter MacDonald of Holmisdale, who spoke simply of the essence of land hunger – 'That we are packed so closely in the place, having so little land, and the land, through constant cultivation refusing to yield crop, and that we would be better off if we had more of the land, so that we could leave some of it out, and so cultivate better; and that if we don't get extended holdings there will be no justice for us . . . If we don't get more land we must needs remain in poverty.'

There were John MacKay of Colbost and John MacSwan of Skinidin, who would tell respectively of 'how we are oppressed by factors and ground officers, who have skinned us' and of how Norman MacRaild had abused his position in those townships to purloin the large offshore grazing islands of Eilean Mhor and Eilean Dubh – 'they always formed part of the township until McRaild deprived the township of them'. There was John Campbell of Hamara, who freely confirmed that he had offered hospitality to Edward McHugh and John Murdoch. There was Alexander MacKenzie of Borreraig on Nicol Martin's remaining section of the estate, who could testify that 'we had to give ten days a year of free labour to Dr Martin, and to cut his corn for him with our own hooks; while a servant of Dr Martin – one William Campbell – who acted as stirk-drover, ploughman, and grieve – in performing this unlawful labour, used to make us work like slaves. The people were in perfect dread of him; and if they did not work as hard as he wished, or were absent for a day, he would threaten them with eviction.'

Such men from all over the broad peninsula had no difficulty in uniting behind the struggle for Waterstein, which was of direct concern only to the crofters of Milovaig and Borrodale. They did so partly from solidarity, and partly because they understood that the matter of Waterstein was inseparable from their own grievances about the lost islands of Skinidin, the forced labour at Borreraig and the unsupportable overcrowding of Holmisdale.

There was dissent in Glendale; there was a minority who, despite John MacPherson's oratory, were covertly or openly

uneasy about the nature of the land struggle. 'The awareness of the dire straits of the people,' says Allan Campbell of
Colbost, 'was reflected in Neil MacLeod's work "Na Croitearan
Sgitheanach", "The Skye Crofters", in which he sympathises
with the people at the loss of the protection of caring chieftains
and the imposition of all manner of restrictions by bailiffs.

'But while MacLeod encourages them to defend their
corner he also advises restraint and the upholding of the law.
Many modern commentators have criticised this, arguing that
MacLeod was merely extending platitudes from the security and
comfort of his Edinburgh base. I don't agree. I think he was
supportive and I believe his recommendation regarding the law
was based on knowledge that the Land League in Glendale had
developed a degree of bullying and summary justice where those
supposed to be less than supportive were given "a doing". It has
been reported that Church leaders were so concerned that four
Free Church ministers met at Hamara in 1882 and advised John
MacPherson and his co-leaders to rein in the land leaguers.'

After nightfall on 5 October 1882 Ewen and Marion MacKenzie,
a middled-aged married couple from Upper Milovaig, paid a visit
to Constable Alex MacVicar at Glendale Police Station. Ewen
MacKenzie, Constable MacVicar subsequently reported to his
superiors, 'was not going with the tenants to attend their meetings,
but sometimes they would compel him to go with them.

'MacKenzie's wife tells me that they are (the tenants)
collecting money among themselves so that if any of them
commits any crime that this money will pay the fine.

'The last meeting that MacKenzie attended was for to get
the shepherds at Waterstein not to interfere with their stock.
MacKenzie also says that they are getting more determined and
vicious, MacKenzie is at present in a dangerous position if he
does not associate with them. They are sure to do him or his
property some harm.'

Constable MacVicar wrote down in English, and forwarded
to Inverness, a statement from Ewen MacKenzie. 'I am a

crofter and fisherman,' the statement read, 'I am 45 years of age, and married. I signed the petition which the tenants of Upper Milivaig and Lower Milivaig presented to the Trustees of Glendale for to get the farm of Waterstein, I withdrew in the month of May last. When I stopped attending their meetings they began to threaten vengeance upon me and again I began to attend their meetings sometimes.

'Tuesday last they had a meeting in the old school house and I did not attend. Thursday night I was hearing whistling about my house and I knew it was the young ones trying to get me out to give me a thrashing. My wife would not allow me out but she went out herself first and I followed her.

'When I went out I saw a man lying at my cornstack and three men above my house and two below it. They were whistling to each other. I am thinking that this man that was at the cornstack was watching me, and whenever he would get ahold of me he would call the rest. I suspect Neil and Archibald Bruce, sons of John Bruce, Hector and Thomas MacLean, sons of Donald MacLean, Malcolm MacPhee son of Margaret Bruce or MacPhee, all from Upper Milivaig, to be the persons watching me on Thursday night. I am now afraid of my life from them and also my property, as they have got a spite at me, and they also threaten me for keeping from the meetings. I am determined not to follow them longer, but unless I get protection from their threats I must join them again to have peace.'

The Bruce brothers were a couple of adult men whose elderly parents, John and Euphemia, had been among the families cleared from Bracadale to overcrowded Milovaig. The teen-aged Malcolm MacPhee's mother Margaret was also a refugee from Bracadale, who was widowed and raising two other small children in Milovaig while officially registered as a pauper. Thomas and Hector MacLean were respectively the 20- and 13-year-old sons of a Milovaig father and a mother from the island of Harris. Their whistling at night almost certainly repre-sented intimidation, but the darker fears of Ewen and Marion

MacKenzie were not realised. Neither they nor their property suffered physical damage and, whatever ill-feeling persisted for however long, the couple continued to live and work and raise five children alongside the Bruces, MacLeans and MacPhees in Upper Milovaig until they died in old age in the 20th century.

Sheriff William Ivory may have hoped for more damning testimony from Glendale. The Battle of the Braes had not improved Sheriff Ivory's opinion of Skye crofters. Not only had he been obliged to flee the scene unceremoniously, skidding footlong over bad trackways in dreadful weather beneath a hail of stones and insults; he had also consequently endured a degree of mockery in the public prints. The *North British Daily Mail* in Glasgow had seized the opportunity to publish a lampoon of 'The Charge of the Light Brigade', Alfred, Lord Tennyson's hit poem of 30 years earlier. Attributed to 'Alfred Tennyson Junior', the 'Charge of the Skye Brigade' read:

> Half a league, half a league!
> Four a-breast – onward!
> All in the valley of Braes
> Marched the half-hundred.
> 'Forward, Police Brigade!
> In front of me,' bold Ivory said;
> Into the valley of Braes
> Charged the half-hundred.
>
> 'Forward, Police Brigade!
> Charge each auld wife and maid!'
> E'en though the Bobbies knew
> Some one had blundered!
> Their's not to make reply;
> Their's not to reason why;
> Their's but to do or die;
> Into the valley of Braes
> Charged the half-hundred.

'Chuckies' to right of them,
'Divots' to left of them,
Women in front of them,
Volleyed and thundered!
Stormed at with stone and shell,
Boldly they charged, they tell,
Down on the Island Host!
Into the mouth of – well!
Charged the half-hundred.

Flourished their batons bare,
Not in the empty air –
Clubbing the lasses there,
Charging the Cailleachs, while
All Scotland wondered!
Plunged in the mist and smoke,
Right thro' the line they broke; –
Cailleach and maiden
Reeled from the baton stroke,
Shattered and sundered;
Then they marched back – intact –
All the half-hundred.

Missiles to right of them,
Brickbats to left of them,
Old wives behind them
Volleyed and floundered.
Stormed at with stone and shell –
Whilst only Ivory fell –
They that had fought so well
Broke thro' the Island Host,
Back from the mouth of – well!
All that was left of them –
All the half-hundred!

> When can their glory fade?
> O, the wild charge they made!
> All Scotland wondered!
> Honour the charge they made!
> Honour the Skye Brigade!
> Donald's half-hundred!

On 21 September 1882 Sheriff William Ivory sat at his desk in Auchindoun in Nairnshire and wrote a long letter to the Police Committee of the County of Inverness requesting that Skye be invaded by a British naval and military expedition.

Ivory's letter was forwarded to J.B. Balfour, MP, in London. The 45-year-old John Blair Balfour was the Liberal Government's Lord Advocate for Scotland, and therefore the chief advisor to the Crown and to the Government on all matters concerning Scottish civil and criminal law. Balfour was a typically astute and accomplished son of the manse in Clackmannan, a graduate of Edinburgh University and had been since 1880 the Liberal Member of Parliament for Clackmannan and Kinross.

'As disturbances have recently taken place in the Island of Skye,' wrote Ivory to his committee, 'and further disturbances are likely to recur, which in my opinion renders the intervention of a naval or military force necessary, I beg to submit to you the following report.

'There are three districts in Skye which may be said to lie in a disturbed state: viz, Braes, Glendale and Kilmuir.

'In all of these a number of crofters about November last refused to pay their rents on the ground that certain grazings were withheld from them, and they still refuse to do so.

'In Kilmuir no serious disturbance has yet taken place. But many of the crofters still refuse to pay their rents, the district is in an unsettled state, and disturbances may occur at any time.

'In Glendale several serious disturbances have already taken place. Besides the refusing to pay their rents the crofters some months ago seized possession of the farm of Waterstein – then

John MacPherson of Lower Milovaig, sketched in the Portree Hotel in
November 1884.

Prime Minister William Ewart Gladstone, 'inclined always to suspect the worst of any aristocracy'. (© National Portrait Gallery, London)

Home Secretary William Harcourt: 'it is all the fault of the silly lairds.' (© National Portrait Gallery, London)

Lord Advocate John Blair Balfour: 'the Government are committed to legislation on the Crofter question.' (© National Portrait Gallery, London)

The young Francis Napier, chairman of the commission of inquiry into
conditions in the Highlands and Islands which would thereafter bear his name.
(© National Portrait Gallery, London)

ABOVE. John Murdoch: 'wrong has been done to the people.'

LEFT. Charles Fraser Mackintosh MP: 'Re-occupation by, and re-distribution among, crofters and cottars of much land now used as large farms will be beneficial to the State, to the owner, and to the occupier.' (Inverness Museum and Art Gallery/Highland Council)

Soldiers and marines are rowed from HMS *Assistance* into Uig Bay on 16 November 1884, guarded by the gunboat HMS *Forester*. (*Illustrated London News*/Mary Evans Picture Library)

The marines first set foot on Skye soil: 'Not a word of disapproval or otherwise was uttered by the few onlookers.' (*Illustrated London News*/Mary Evans Picture Library)

Transferring officers from boat to boat at Uig quay. (*Illustrated London News*/Mary Evans Picture Library)

Marines march up and over the Trotternish Ridge from Uig into Staffin.
(*Illustrated London News*/Mary Evans Picture Library)

Sheriff William Ivory, in a white coat, instructs his police officers to build a
crossing for the marines over a Skye burn. (*Illustrated London News*/
Mary Evans Picture Library)

Right. A local elder begins the crofters' meeting on Cnoc an t-Sithein with a prayer. (*Illustrated London News*/Mary Evans Picture Library)

As the marines approach Glendale, John MacPherson addresses his fellow crofters: 'Be courageous and not afraid ... no matter how many policemen and marines the Government might send.' (*Illustrated London News*/Mary Evans Picture Library)

in the hands of the proprietor – drove off his shepherds and cattle; and placed their own cattle on the farm instead. The proprietor thereupon obtained an Interdict from the Court of Session forbidding the crofters to interfering with him in his possession of the farm. At this time the greater number of the able-bodied crofters were absent at the Fishing on the East Coast; and the others who remained behind removed their cattle from the farm in obedience to the interdict, but at the same time threatened that when the other crofters returned, they would set the interdict at defiance.

'The greater number of the men have now returned to Glendale, and within the last few days the crofters have by means of threats and intimidation driven the proprietor's shepherds off the farm, and it is thought that in a very short time – if they have not already done so – they will place their cattle again on the farm in defiance of the Interdict.'

Sheriff Ivory then provided a description of the incidents and the trial which had preceded and followed the Battle of the Braes in April. Although the five Braes crofters under summonses had been apprehended during the struggle, 'no proceedings' had been pursued against their friends and neighbours, who during the Battle of the Braes had 'seriously injured' four of the Glasgow policemen and their captain.

'But this leniency on the part of the authorities,' continued Ivory, 'did no good. The crofters continued openly to refuse payment of their rents and subsequently placed their cattle on Ben-lea, and they still insist on keeping them there . . .'

Further orders of the Court of Session were therefore due to be served on 'between 50 and 60' Skye crofters, and Sheriff Ivory was at a loss to know how this could be accomplished. 'The Inverness-shire Police force is quite inadequate by itself to such a duty.' After its experience in April, the Glasgow Police Force was reluctant to involve itself again in Skye – 'difficulties may be anticipated with the Glasgow Town Council in procuring the necessary force . . .'

After 'careful consideration', Lord Lovat, the Lord Lieutenant of Inverness-shire, and Sheriff William Ivory had concurred that the best solution was to employ 'a naval or military force' in Skye.

'[In] such remote and disturbed districts,' wrote Ivory, 'where all the crofters reside close to the sea-shore a gun boat with an adequate naval force would be the best to employ ... the messenger at arms, Police and naval force could be landed within a very short distance of the crofters' houses instead of having to march 24 miles in the case of the Braes and 70 miles in the case of Glendale exposed to the attacks of a hostile population ... Further the sudden landing of a force on their shores without previous notice and due knowledge that such landing might be reported to them whenever it was required would probably have the salutory effect of impressing the crofters with the hopelessness of defying the authorities of the law.'

His proposal contained difficulties, admitted Sheriff Ivory. 'I understand ... that the Admiralty object to the use of a naval force for the above purpose on the ground that a great many naval Coast Volunteers [naval reservists] come from the Western Islands. I doubt however whether any such volunteers come from Skye. I believe the greater number come from Lewis, Harris and other Islands of the outer Hebrides. As, however, I understand it is thought better not to make use of a naval force the only other force that can be employed is the Military ... I propose at once making a requisition to the General commanding the forces in Scotland for 100 soldiers to act as a protection and aid to the civil authorities ...'

The response from Lord Advocate Balfour to this petition to deploy British armed forces against British citizens came 12 days later. It was a qualified rejection. Balfour wrote directly to Sheriff Ivory from Whitehall on 3 November 1882. He accepted that messengers-at-arms in Skye were 'entitled to have adequate protection ... the question to be determined is, by whom should that protecting force be provided, and should it consist of Police or of Soldiers?'

Soldiers, ruled Balfour, 'should not be employed upon Police duty which is likely to be of a continuing character . . . [It] seems to be the view of the Authorities in Skye that the force would require to remain in the Island for a considerable time.

'These considerations have led the Government to the conclusion that they ought not to sanction the employment of a military force under existing circumstances, but that the County Authorities should provide or obtain the services of such a force of Police as they may consider necessary . . . It is not for the Government to prescribe or even to suggest the particular mode in which the County Authorities should fulfil this duty, whether by adding to their own Police Force, or by temporarily obtaining the services of Police from other Counties or Burghs, but I am authorised by [the Home Secretary] Sir William Harcourt to say, that if they should resolve to make an addition to the number of their own police, he will be ready to grant his consent . . . to whatever addition they may consider requisite.'

As the winter of 1882 dragged on towards the dawn of 1883, the county authorities of Inverness-shire attempted to build a large and powerful police force on the foundation of a small number of placid Highland officers which was incapable of or unwilling to quell insurrections in the island of Skye. Within his own terms of reference, William Ivory had been right. The situation in Skye required a paramilitary squad of counter-insurgents, not young Constable Alexander MacVicar from North Uist.

Such a squad, they quickly discovered, could not be recruited locally. On 6 December 1882 William Grant, the clerk to Inverness Police Committee, circulated to his members, to Lord Advocate John Blair Balfour and to Home Secretary William Harcourt the information that 'although the County have recently resolved to add 50 men to their force, these men, even when obtained, will be quite untrained and inefficient, and most

of them unavailable for such difficult service for some considerable time.'

Moreover, William Ivory had been correct to point out
that the Glasgow city fathers were reluctant to send their own
policemen 200 miles north on another humiliating errand. The
same reluctance pertained outside Glasgow. Is it true, asked
Sir Donald Macfarlane, then MP for Carlow, in the House of
Commons on 24 November, 'as reported in the *North British
Daily Mail*, that the magistrates of Edinburgh, Govan, and
Partick, and other places, have refused the assistance of their
police for the protection of officers engaged in serving writs of
ejectment upon crofters in Skye; and, if he can state the reasons
given for such refusals by the magistrates referred to?'

'I understand,' replied Lord Advocate Balfour stiffly, 'that in
some cases the requests for assistance have been granted, and
in some refused; but I have no information as to the grounds of
refusal.'

When Lanarkshire Police Committee agreed to send a few
dozen officers to Skye, far from doing so in a spirit of comradely
cooperation with a brother force, they offered their men in the
clear understanding that they were reluctant to perform the
dirty work of Highland landowners – and if Inverness wished
them to do so, Inverness would pay through the nose. Lanark's
conditions, which William Grant described as 'onerous', were
that the County of Inverness would compensate the Lanarkshire
police force for every small expenditure. Inverness would pay all
travel costs and would pay for 'due and healthy accommodation
and subsistence'. If the Lanarkshire superintendent considered
that his men were not being adequately fed and housed by the
Inverness-shire authorities, he reserved the right to arrange
their meals and beds himself and the cost 'shall be reimbursed
by the County of Inverness'. Inverness would pay Lanark for
their officers' clothing as well as wages from the moment the
men left Lanarkshire until the moment they returned. If any
pension or compensation was due to a Lanarkshire police officer

or his family 'in consequence of injury or death resulting from this special service' in Skye, then Inverness would pay every last penny.

Even while agreeing to such conditions, by early December 1882 Inverness Police Committee could raise only 135 policemen from the whole of the rest of Scotland. If they added 35 of their own bobbies, as they could ill afford to do, they had a grand total of 170 officers to send west. '[A] force of 170 men,' wrote William Grant from his office in Inverness Castle, 'is wholly inadequate to to enforce the law in the disturbed districts of Skye, where there are threats of opposing the officers of the law by armed bodies, and that such an expedition may cause riot and bloodshed.'

It may have been some consolation to William Grant to realise that the 'disturbances' in Skye were beginning to cause as many headaches at Westminster as they did in Inverness Castle.

SEVEN

A Little Ireland in Skye

DEMANDS FOR A special inquiry into Highland unrest had been made, and rebuffed, since the 1870s. Members of metropolitan Gaelic and Highland associations, as well as reformers such as John Murdoch and some politicians, hoped that an impartial and penetrating public inquiry would lay bare the true nature of the society which had been permitted to develop in the Highlands and Islands during the 19th century.

In 1877 Alexander MacKenzie of the *Celtic Magazine* attended a public meeting held at Inverness Music Hall by the reformist MP for Inverness Burghs, Charles Fraser Mackintosh. MacKenzie was then the 38-year-old upwardly mobile son of a crofter from Gairloch on the west coast of Ross-shire. A persistent, pugnacious and extraordinarily energetic man, he became Dean of Guild, or building control officer, for the burgh of Inverness. There he settled on the west bank of the River Ness with his English wife and their young family, and devoted himself not only to enforcing building regulations but also to writing a series of clan and other Highland histories. His *Celtic Magazine* was originally a typical Celtic revivalist publication of its time which devoted its bilingual pages to folklore, verse and shinty. As the land struggle progressed, both MacKenzie and his magazine became increasingly political and increasingly devoted to the crofters' cause. Like John Murdoch, MacKenzie was a stalwart of the Gaelic Society of Inverness who helped to establish that organisation's early, radical character.

On that day in Inverness Music Hall Alexander MacKenzie took the opportunity to ask Fraser Mackintosh, 'amid the general laughter of the audience', whether, 'Keeping in view that the Government has graciously considered the reputed scarcity of crabs and lobsters, and of herrings and garvies, on our Highland coast, of sufficient importance to justify them in granting two separate Royal Commissions of Inquiry, will you, in your place in Parliament, next session, move that a similar Commission be granted to inquire into the present impoverished and wretched condition and, in some places, the scarcity of men and women in the Highlands; the cause of this state of things; and the most effectual remedy for ameliorating the condition of the Highland Crofters generally?'

Fraser Mackintosh was reported at the time to have replied that: 'A Member of Parliament had a certain power, and only a certain power. The question which was here raised was a very large one, and he did not think that he would have the slightest chance of getting such a Commission as was referred to, unless the Government was prepared for the demand beforehand, and unless the request was strengthened by a general expression of feeling in its favour throughout the country. If Mr Mackenzie, who had written an able article on the subject, which had attracted great attention, and others with him, could by petition, or by deputation to the Prime Minister, pave the way for a motion, he would be very glad to make it. His moving in the matter without adequate support would hamper and hurt the laudable object Mr Mackenzie had at heart.'

Following 1877 the 'general expression of feeling in favour' of such a Commission had grown. The Gaelic Society of Inverness supported the notion. The Invernesians were joined by the Federation of Celtic Societies, the Gaelic Society of Perth and the Highland Land Reform Associations of Inverness and Edinburgh. In 1880 Charles Fraser Mackintosh himself came round to the idea. Once light was shone upon the true state of Highland affairs, reasoned those campaigners, legislation to balance the scales of justice could not fail to follow.

They were right. Thanks to the people of Braes and, most immediately, Glendale, that is exactly what happened.

Parliament was not ignorant of the subject. In June 1881 Dr Charles Cameron of the *North British Daily Mail*, wearing his other hat as a Member of Parliament for Glasgow, stood up in the House of Commons to ask Home Secretary William Harcourt if he was aware of the trouble in Kilmuir – 'Whether his attention has been called to the threatened eviction of sixteen families of Highland crofters, embracing nearly one hundred persons, from their holdings in the Island of Skye; and, whether, taking into account the recent frequency of such evictions in the Highlands of Scotland, Government will consider the propriety of extending to the Highland crofter population protection against arbitrary dispossession similar to that which the Law affords in the case of copyholders in England and small tenant farmers in Ireland?'

Harcourt brushed the matter off, replying that he 'had no information except a newspaper paragraph which had been sent to him on the subject; and, knowing how inaccurate statements of that kind affecting private persons might be, he did not think it right to express any judgment on the matter until he was in possession of information of a really authentic character'.

The Battle of the Braes provoked several questions in the House. On the day after the event, 20 April 1882, Charles Fraser Mackintosh asked Lord Advocate J.B. Balfour, 'If he can explain the circumstances under which fifty of the Glasgow Police Force have been sent to the Island of Skye; and, whether this step has been taken with his sanction, and on whom the cost will fall?'

Balfour replied that 'for several months past the crofters – small tenants – at Braes, in the Island of Skye, have refused to pay any rent unless on condition of getting back a piece of hill grazing of which they say they were deprived some 17 or 18 years ago. In consequence of the crofters taking this position, Lord Macdonald, the proprietor, or his factor, sent a Sheriff's officer to Braes, on the 7th of this month, to serve summonses for the payment of rent, and also summonses for removal upon crofters.

'The Sheriff's officer was accompanied by an assistant, and also by a ground officer in the employment of Lord Macdonald. When they came to Braes, they were met and stopped by about 150 persons, who assaulted them, took from the Sheriff's officer the summonses, burned them on the spot, and at the same time threatened the officer with more serious violence if he returned. It was a clear case of premeditated assault on an officer executing a legal warrant, and I accordingly directed that four or five of the ringleaders who had been named should be apprehended and tried.

'The authorities of the county – Inverness-shire – stated that they believed that the force of constables at their disposal might not be adequate for the apprehension of the offenders, and they therefore applied to the police authorities at Glasgow for aid, under the provisions of the Glasgow Police Act, and the Glasgow authorities gave the services of the constables in regard to whom the Question is asked. These steps were taken with my approval, and the offenders were apprehended and lodged in prison yesterday morning with a view to their trial. The cost will fall on the county of Inverness-shire, as the constables were required for the vindication of the law in that county.'

Joseph Biggar, the Irish Nationalist MP for Cavan and treas-urer of the Irish Land League, wanted to know if the police sent to Braes had been 'armed with revolvers'. Balfour replied that they had not been armed – 'They had no weapons other than their ordinary bâtons.'

All of which led inevitably to the heart of the matter. Donald Macfarlane was yet another Irish MP whose sympathies lay with Home Rule and the land struggle. In 1885 Macfarlane would be elected as MP for Argyllshire, making him Scotland's first Roman Catholic Member of Parliament. In 1882 he was still the Nationalist MP for Carlow in Ireland. In that capacity, on 28 April 1882, while the five Braes crofters were on trial in Inverness and while the people of Milovaig and Borrodale in Glendale were being surreptitiously denied the lease of Waterstein Farm, Donald Macfarlane put a question directly to the Prime Minister, William Ewart Gladstone.

Macfarlane wanted to know if Gladstone's 'attention has been called to the state of feeling existing amongst the Crofters in the Island of Skye; and, if he proposes to ascertain, by the appointment of a Commission, or by any other means, the condition and grievances of the Crofters in that Island, the other Western Islands, and the Orkney and Shetland groups?'

Gladstone prevaricated. 'Sir,' he replied, 'this is a Question of a serious nature, and I do not feel that I could answer it advantageously in the form of a reply to a Question. I think that a Notice has been given upon the subject, in which it will be raised in more convenient form; and the Government will, before that Notice comes on, carefully consider the whole matter, and give Parliament the view we take.'

John Dick Peddie, the Liberal member for Kilmarnock Burghs in the Scottish Lowlands, protested that 'considering the importance of the Question, and the state of matters in Skye' the question of a commission of inquiry should be more urgently addressed.

Gladstone brushed Peddie smoothly aside. 'Sir,' he said, 'if it were in my power to add to the manufactures of this country, I would, in the first place, add the manufacture of time. Unfortunately, it is not in my power . . . I heartily wish I could give any such assistance; but it is not in my power.'

In 1882 William Gladstone was 72 years old and two years into his second period of office as Liberal Prime Minister of the United Kingdom. Although he had been born in Liverpool, educated at Eton College and Oxford University, lived for most of his life in Wales and represented a Scottish constituency only for the last 15 of his 63 years in the House of Commons, Gladstone would correctly insist that 'not a drop of blood in my veins is not Scottish'. His father was a merchant from Leith, the port of Edinburgh, and his mother came from the market town of Dingwall in the Highlands.

Gladstone's second administration, between 1880 and 1885, was dominated by two issues which would, almost incidentally, have enormous repercussions in the Highlands and Islands of Scotland. As one of its many attempts to answer the Irish Question, in 1881 Gladstone's Government passed an Irish Land Act which, among other things, gave Irish smallholders and tenant farmers security of tenure and officially adjudicated rents. In 1884 it multiplied the rural franchise through the Third Reform Act, which gave adult male agricultural workers and agrarian householders the vote. That measure enfranchised around 6,000,000 men throughout rural Britain. The 6,000,000 included almost every crofter over the age of 21 in the north and west of Scotland.

James Hunter has written that William Gladstone was 'inclined always to suspect the worst of any aristocracy', and that he 'tended instinctively to take the crofting population's side'. That is true, and would be borne out by epochal events in the middle of the 1880s. The older that Gladstone became, the more fiercely was he informed by an evangelical sense of right and wrong, of justice and injustice, and the more motivated he became by a Christian moral prerogative to use power to assist the weak, the poor, the downtrodden and the disenfranchised.

He was also a politician to his core. However inclined he personally may have been to take the crofters' side, William Gladstone was fully aware of the great powers ranged against them within both Scottish society and the Palace of Westminster. He knew that what was happening to Scottish Gaels in the 19th century was little more than an extension of the Enclosures which had dispossessed the English peasantry in the preceding two centuries, which had in turn led to immense increases in agricultural production and fed the Industrial Revolution. A special, exceptionalist case must be made for Scottish Highlanders if they were to win exemption from the rule of law and market forces. While, as he told John Dick Peddie, his Government had its hands full with other matters, in April 1882 William Gladstone thought it best to wait for the appropriate moment to show his hand.

In November 1882, while Sheriff Ivory and the Inverness-shire Police Committee were trawling Scotland in search of reinforcements to send to Skye, Donald Macfarlane repeated his question to the Prime Minister, asking if 'he can now state whether it is the intention of Her Majesty's Government to appoint a Royal Commission to inquire into and report upon the causes which have led to disturbances in Skye . . . and other parts of Scotland; and, whether, in the event of Her Majesty's Government having decided against the appointment of a Commission, he will, before the House rises, give a day for the discussion of the question?'

No, said Gladstone. '[We] hear reports of a different kind tending towards popular commotion, that matters are in such a state as to render it peculiarly incumbent on the Government to consider very carefully what course it may be proper to take, in order to avoid any steps which might possibly lead to inconven-ient consequences.

'The hon. Member will recollect that the difficulty in Skye at the present moment occurs under these circumstances – that there are legal rights in contest between one and more proprie-tors and a number of tenants, that the natural course would be that these rights should be ascertained; but that at present there is an appearance of resistance to the first step towards ascer-taining – namely, the service of writs, or whatever the proper name may be for that step in Scotland.

'With regard to the appointment of a Commission, the hon. Member will recollect that there was an opportunity for full discussion of this matter in the summer, when my right hon. and learned Friend the Lord Advocate stated, on the part of the Government, the reasons which led them to believe that it would not be wise to issue a Royal Commission on the subject. On the facts placed before them, Her Majesty's Government cannot see in anything any reason for departing from that determination.

'Of course, if we are in that state of mind, it almost follows that I must answer the latter part of the hon. Gentleman's Question in the negative, and say that we are not prepared before the House rises to give a day for the discussion of this subject. With regard to any apparent importunity on the part of the hon. Gentleman, I beg him to believe that nothing could be further from my intention than to make any charge against him on that subject. I am sure he does it from an earnest and philanthropic interest in the matter.'

Two days after Gladstone's response to Donald Macfarlane's question, on 30 November 1882, the Liberal member for Kirkcaldy Burghs, Sir George Campbell, a former Lieutenant-Governor of Bengal, wondered 'Whether Her Majesty's Government will consider the possibility of giving to the remnant of the Celtic population of Scotland the same legal recognition of their ancient rights in the land which has been so liberally granted to the Irish?'

Before Gladstone could reply the Conservative MP for Bute, Sir Charles Dalrymple, forced the other side of the argument, asking the Prime Minister 'if he was aware that one of the most important points in dispute between the Skye crofters and one of the largest landed proprietors in Skye [in Braes] had just been settled by friendly arrangement; and, whether he did not think that such an arrangement so made was better than vague suggestions about ancient rights, or any interference by Parliament?'

'The intelligence to which the hon. Member opposite has referred has not reached me;' said Gladstone, 'but I receive it with great satisfaction. I was about to have answered my hon. Friend that the relative rights of parties were so far in course of

progress towards being fixed that the first step had been taken
on the part of the landlords for the purpose of having them fixed;
and that I did not think that a period like that, when difficulty
attended that step and the actual execution of the law, was the
time for raising any question of the nature of the Question; but
I receive with great satisfaction what has been stated by the hon.
Gentleman . . . With the greatest possible respect to the hon.
Member, and to the hon. Gentleman opposite, I think I may say
the House will feel that I must wait for some further and more
definite statement on the subject before I undertake to answer
anything of the nature of the Question put to me just now.'

On 15 December 1882 Lord Advocate John Blair Balfour
met Home Secretary William Harcourt in London to discuss
the matter of a police or military intervention in Skye. Their
conference represented an extraordinary amount of time and
mental energy devoted by senior members of the Government
to agrarian unrest in the north-west of Scotland. Baffled by, and
vaguely impatient with, the inability of Inverness to deal with
its own internal difficulties, Balfour then wrote to William Ivory
requesting specific and detailed information.

The Lord Advocate and the Home Secretary wanted the
Sheriff of Inverness-shire to enlighten them on nine particular
points. They wished to know 'for what specific services in what
particular places' Government assistance was required, as well
as 'the amount and character of the assistance sought'. They
required evidence to support William Grant's earlier assertion
that 'a force of 170 men is wholly inadequate to enforce the law
in the disturbed districts in Skye'. They wanted to know what
was being done with the extra few dozen police officers which
Inverness-shire had recently acquired; how many policemen
were currently assigned to duty in which parts of Skye; and
whether or not the 'question' between Lord Macdonald and the
crofters of Braes had been settled.

Balfour and Harcourt asked Ivory how many policemen were
presently on duty in Braes and Glendale, and what attempts had

been made by the police to protect the shepherds employed on Waterstein Farm 'from molestation by the crofters'.

If Balfour and Harcourt were baffled, William Ivory was exasperated. Ivory scribbled in the margins of his letter from Balfour such phrases as 'Glendale, 25 or 26 men accused of assaulting a shepherd – breach of interdict (roughly 2,000 of population) 450 able-bodied men, as many women. They say they will go as far as sticks and stones will carry them, no farther so won't use firearms but will use sythes [sic] – generally believed in the country and so does constable report . . .'

Ivory and his police committee then despatched the newly appointed Chief Constable of Inverness-shire, a 43–year-old named Alexander 'Alisdair' McHardy who took up his new post at Inverness Castle only on 26 December 1882, to Skye to gather detailed answers to the questions from London. McHardy, a native Gaelic speaker from Braemar in Aberdeenshire who had previously served in Sutherland, walked into an unenviable position. His predecessor had resigned two months earlier, leaving a substantial amount of unfinished business – not least the troubles in Skye and the appointment of extra officers to police the island. Alexander McHardy barely had time to warm his office seat before he was thrust into the fray.

Following his field expedition to Skye in late December 1882, Chief Constable McHardy reported to the procurator fiscal in Inverness, who in his turn prepared 'the following observations' for Balfour and Harcourt in early January 1883. The Government of the United Kingdom was being asked to protect officers of the law when serving writs in Braes, and 'to protect the Police in apprehending parties at Glendale who were accused of assaulting shepherds in charge of stock on Waterstein, and of Breach of Interdict'.

The 'amount and character' of the assistance requested was as previously stated – 'send a Government steamer and marines to the Island accompanied by a body of Constables, the steamer being kept in the locality for some time so as to overawe the people'. It was pointed out that a body of 50 police officers had barely been able to execute their orders in Braes. 'In respect of Glendale the people there publicly avowed and continue openly to say that while they will receive any writs offered them they will resist any force sent to deprive them of Waterstein and that they will go as far as sticks and stones will carry them in resistance.

'Moreover it is believed altho there is no proof of it that the people there are arming themselves with scythes as the Braes people have done and they have mutually agreed to assist each other. Dealing with a population of over 2,000 people actuated by the spirit indicated by these facts, the Committee felt that 170 men, especially men not drilled or accustomed to act together would be wholly inadequate to enforce the law within the disturbed districts . . . the Chief Constable . . . after making careful enquiries on the ground, reported that as regards Glendale alone 170 Constables would be quite inadequate unless they were armed for self-defence and that he firmly believed that serious personal injuries and bloodshed would be the result of enforcing the law in the district. Sheriff Speirs and the procurator fiscal of Skye agree with the Chief Constable.'

Chief Constable McHardy was, in the early days of 1883, urgently attempting to complete the recruitment of 50 extra policemen. Fifty officers would therefore be sent to Skye 'so soon as the arrangements can be completed'. In the meantime, said the procurator fiscal in Inverness, there were 11 constables in Skye: 'viz, Portree 3 Constables. Carbost 1. Broadford 1. Isleornsay 1. Edinbane 1. Dunvegan 1. Glendale 1. Uig 1. Staffin 1.' There was not a police officer among the '300 to 400' people of Braes, whose difficulties with Lord Macdonald had 'recently been settled and everything is at present quiet'. In conversation with Chief Constable McHardy on 30 December 1882, however, Lord Macdonald's factor Alexander MacDonald had stated 'that he did not expect the peace to be lasting and that a recurrence of the agitation would take place before long'.

It was admitted to London that the population and area of Glendale was 'not accurately known'. It was 'variously stated at from 1,500 to 2,000 people and the district is about 12 miles in length and from 1 mile to 2½ miles in breadth.'

And finally, 'No attempt has been made to protect by Police Agency the shepherds at Waterstein beyond the protection afforded by the one Constable who was sent to the district for the purpose. As already stated there is no accommodation for Constables at Glendale and the people were unwilling to give a room for the one Constable.'

Balfour and Harcourt received this information early in January 1883. They deliberated for as long as possible. Their hands would soon be forced.

On 11 January 1883 the Court of Session in Edinburgh, sitting under Lord Glencorse, refused to utilise the Royal Mail to summon to their bar five crofters from Glendale. Instead, the 55–year-old messenger-at-arms Donald MacTavish was sent from Glasgow to Skye to deliver the summonses in the traditional manner, by hand.

Inverness County Police was informed that Donald MacTavish expected to carry his wand of peace into Glendale on 17 January. Matters were clearly moving towards a climax, even if nobody – from Lower Milovaig to Westminster – could yet be sure what form that culmination would take. On 15 January Chief Constable Alexander McHardy sent a note from Inverness to the police in Portree telling them of his intention to send to Glendale a handful of experienced officers from the mainland, firstly to pave the way for the arrival of the messenger-at-arms and thereafter to uphold the law in such places as Waterstein.

McHardy immediately received a reply from the Sheriff-Substitute Peter Speirs in Portree House. Peter Alexander Speirs had been born in 1842 in Cawnpore in British India. He was no longer in Cawnpore when he was 15 years old, having been sent back to Britain ten years earlier. The young Speirs returned first to Stirling in Scotland, where he was raised and tutored at home by five maiden aunts who were his father's sisters, before qualifying as an advocate and eventually becoming sheriff-substitute in Skye.

If the 15-year-old Peter Speirs had still been in Cawnpore in the summer of 1857 he almost certainly would not have survived the year, let alone lived to marry a woman from Newcastle-upon-Tyne and be employed as sheriff-substitute in Portree in 1883. As Speirs and most of his countrymen were fully aware, Cawnpore had been a bloodbath during the Indian Rebellion – which they knew as the Indian Mutiny – of 1857. All but seven of 1,200 British soldiers and civilians, including women and children, in Cawnpore were massacred by rebel Sepoy troops and irregulars. The place of Peter Alexander Speirs' birth remained throughout the 19th century a byword for the collapse of British law and order and the brutal triumph of indigenous insurrection.

It is possible that Peter Speirs moved to Skye at least partly to put as much distance as possible between himself and the blood, heat and anarchy of British India. It is certain that he was disturbed to discover in that Hebridean island such anti-establishment sentiments and activities as had led to barbarity in Cawnpore. He was an educated and reasonable man, but his incredulous and uneasy responses to the events in Skye in 1882 and 1883 cannot be divorced from the horrific news that, as a teenager in Britain, he had received from the town of his infancy in India.

'There is no other place,' wrote Speirs to Chief Constable McHardy on 15 January, a day before it was proposed to send a small detachment of mainland policemen into Glendale, 'for the Glendale [police]men to put up than at Hamara Lodge, and as it is for the benefit of the proprietor that these men are being sent, he is bound to put them up – At Dunvegan the two extra men will easily find quarters.

'I fear,' continued Speirs to McHardy, 'that the Glendale people are very determined, these Glasgow "advisers" are keeping up the agitation – however I do not anticipate any row tomorrow, and advised Inspector Macdonald [of Portree] to state at once that they were not going to arrest anyone, merely to reside in the district as ordered. I also suggested that if the Messenger at Arms went, he would be more likely to serve his citations without police, than with them, and that he should have other (civil) witnesses.

'A crisis must come soon now, I suppose – I wish to goodness it could be avoided – but I am certain these [Glendale] men will not give in . . .

'I suggested to Inspector Macdonald that the Steamer at Glendale and Dunvegan might be watched occasionally, in case any rifles be arrived – they would surely not think of putting anything in the way of torpedos in Loch Pooltiel, being afraid of their own boats . . .

'Your notion of the double patrol is very good. I shall anxiously await the news of the parties reception – but tho noisy perhaps don't expect it will be offensive.'

By 'torpedos', in 1883 Sheriff-substitute Speirs was referring to mines or any other underwater booby-traps. He was right to suppose that no such devices would be laid by the Glendale militants, in Loch Pooltiel or anywhere else. His fears of smuggled rifles were equally unfounded. Peter Speirs' reluctance to 'anticipate any row tomorrow' was however overly optimistic. The 'crisis' would come sooner than he feared.

On Tuesday, 16 January 1883, six 'experienced' policemen from the Inverness-shire mainland made their way north-west from Portree in the company of Inspector Malcolm Macdonald. Two of them were to augment the single constable in Dunvegan; the other four were to continue to Hamara Lodge in the heart of Glendale and from those headquarters to assist Constable Alexander MacVicar in the execution of his duties. They came from Kingussie and Aviemore, Inverness and Strathglass, and they were quite unfamiliar with the Skye terrain – they had earlier been disappointed to learn that no one-inch to one-mile maps of Glendale had yet been printed.

In Glendale, Constable MacVicar became suddenly a hapless witness to unprecedented events. 'I was at Station the time the Milivaig and Glendale tenants got the warning that they [the policemen] were coming,' MacVicar would report. 'The horn was blowing in all directions and the people running towards the road throughout the glen.

'I saw the Milivaig tenants running past, each of them armed with new sticks made for the purpose.

'I did not know what was going on and I walked after the Milivaig tenants towards the Post Office and I then saw the crowd after passing the Post Office and also found out the affair. In an hour's time there were about 800 assembled from the two estates and some from the estate of MacLeod of MacLeod.

'After the crowd disappeared on the top of the Glen about 300 gathered who were late in getting the warning.'

As Constable MacVicar must at least have surmised, the crowd of 'about 800' which disappeared into Cnoc an t-Sìthein beyond Fasach was in hot pursuit of his fellow police officers. Inspector Macdonald had left his two new policemen in Dunvegan before proceeding to Glendale with the other four, reinforced and guided by the resident Dunvegan constable. That party of six uniformed officers walked around the head of Loch Dunvegan, past Skinidin and Colbost and over into Glendale itself.

A few hours later, at 7.00 in the evening, Chief Constable Alexander McHardy received in Inverness a telegram from Inspector Macdonald, who was by then back in Dunvegan. 'When near Hamara Lodge,' read the telegram, 'self and Constables attacked by excited crowd, about four hundred, self, MacKenzie, Boyd, Cameron kicked, thrown to ground, all roughly handled, forced for six miles, several times assaulted, none seriously injured all more or less, wire instructions, full report will follow.'

From the crofters' point of view, the incident was worthy of commemoration in song. The Milovaig bard Donald MacLean,

the father of the two young men who had earlier been accused
of harassing their neighbour Ewen MacKenzie when the latter
disassociated himself from their cause, promptly wrote 'Thainig
Sgeulachd gu ar Baile' ('Word Came to our Township'):

Word came to our township
that the police were coming to catch us,
coming into the glen at full speed,
and that checked our high spirits.

The Great Horn was sounded,
the pipers began to tune their drones,
and I heard an old woman shouting,
'The Children of the Gaels, Oh, they won't retreat!'

Although it was frightening, we had to move
and to hold our ground with hard courage;
there was one with a stick, one with a flail,
and one with a club made from a sooty rafter.

What a beautiful sight that was,
advancing up the brae of Fasach,
banners fluttering from high staffs
and waving gently in the wind.

Brave heroes came to our assistance,
all of one mind to accompany us –
the men of Skinidin and Colbost,
as fully armed as ourselves.

We drove them off as they deserved,
sending them over the boundary of the estate;
when we reached the public house,
night had come upon us, and we were tired.

In the light of those assaults, the decision of messenger-at-arms Donald MacTavish to walk on the following morning into Glendale to serve summonses on five Milovaig crofters was both courageous and foolish. He had, however, taken the same path before without encountering obstruction or incurring physical harm. Interdicts and court edicts had been served on Glendale crofters since the summer of the previous year, forbidding them from trespassing or pasturing their animals on Waterstein farm and ordering them to stop harassing estate shepherds. Those interdicts, some of which had been delivered by MacTavish himself, had then simply been ignored and had presumably found their way onto peat fires.

Once he had fulfilled his obligations by handing on the court orders, Donald MacTavish and the Glendale crofters had on those occasions bidden each other cordial farewells. Alexander Mackenzie of the *Celtic Magazine* asserted that very far from obstructing the messenger-at-arms, Glendale crofters had at times actually helped him to serve his interdicts – 'On the last occasion they, with the greatest consideration, ferried Mr MacTavish, the sheriff officer [*sic*], across the loch from one district to another with the unserved portion of the writs, for those on the opposite side, in his possession.'

Donald MacTavish may therefore have presumed that he would be spared on Wednesday the violence which was inflicted on police officers on Tuesday. He may have assumed that the greater part of the Glendale crofters' rage had been spent on protesting against their district coming under police occupation – especially, as had been the case in Braes, when the policemen were foreigners. Even Sheriff William Ivory would admit that 'nothing gave such great offence to the crofters and their friends as the sending . . . a large force of strange police to Skye'. MacTavish was also, as a messenger-at-arms must be, a hard man. He walked upright into the no-go zone. Later that day, having counted his bruises in the Dunvegan Hotel, he could pride himself on having tried to do his duty.

On Thursday, 18 January, 'a body of about 2,000 people followed [Donald MacTavish] all the way to Dunvegan, a distance of 10 miles, to compel him to leave the district. Learning that he had already left for Portree, the people soon dispersed and returned peaceably to their homes.' Constable Alexander MacVicar was once again the sole representative of the law permitted by the district's residents to remain in Glendale.

Twenty-two days into his new job, Chief Constable Alexander McHardy was furious. Glendale had effectively declared itself an autonomous community, in which the only laws were those of a broad consensus of the population, and where any attempt to impose an external jurisdiction would be resisted with force.

Upon receiving Inspector Macdonald's telegram from Dunvegan on the evening of 16 January describing the rout of his officers in Glendale earlier that day, Chief Constable McHardy replied instantly, telling Malcolm Macdonald to remain for the moment in Dunvegan. (Almost as an afterthought, the Chief Constable also asked after the well-being of Constable Alexander MacVicar, who was still keeping his head diplomatically below the parapet out in Glendale and who had not been mentioned in Macdonald's telegram.)

McHardy then wired Sheriff Ivory with the latest appalling news before sitting down to write to his police committee members. 'The state of matters at Glendale,' wrote McHardy, 'is now so determined and serious that I do not hesitate in saying that any force other than an armed force would be quite useless and unsafe. Any unarmed body of less than from 250 to 300 Constables would certainly be quite inadequate.

'The attack on the Inspector and five Constables who were sent to that district to do ordinary patrol duty and reside there, and not for the purpose of executing any Warrant of apprehension or serving any Writs shows that the minds of the people have become corrupted and the district assumed a state of revolt.'

William Ivory, who was more convinced than ever of the strength of his case for sending either armed police or preferably a military detachment into Skye, quickly passed all of this on to Lord Advocate Balfour in London. Ivory continued to mistake the sentiments of his superiors. After consideration, Balfour, Home Secretary William Harcourt and Prime Minister William Gladstone elected once more neither to arm the Inverness-shire police nor to despatch Royal Marines to Skye.

Instead, before making a momentous announcement in the House of Commons, they sent a civil servant to Glendale.

EIGHT

The Crofters Dictate the Terms of their Arrest

A S HIS NAME SUGGESTS, Malcolm MacNeill's paternal
line was of the Hebrides. His father was Alexander,
the 5th MacNeill of Colonsay. Although his mother was an
Englishwoman and his wife was from Edinburgh, Malcolm
had been born in the island of Jura. He spent his early life with
his five siblings in Colonsay. He was then packed off to Eton
and Sandhurst and spent some time in New Zealand before
returning to Scotland and settling in Edinburgh. The fact
that he remained a Gaelic speaker in adulthood was, as much
as anything else, testament to the continuing ubiquity of the
language in 19th-century Scotland.

In early 1883 Malcolm MacNeill was 42 years old and living
in considerable comfort with his young family in a large house
in the New Town of Edinburgh. He was also a visiting officer
to the central Board of Supervision, a function which he owed at
least in part to the fact that his uncle, Sir John MacNeill, was the
Board's founding chairman. It nonetheless put him in a position
to influence the quality of poor relief to the able-bodied destitute throughout Scotland. MacNeill would continue to occupy
similar, if increasingly elevated roles, throughout his career,
becoming finally the vice-president of the Local Government
Board for Scotland, an appointed executive position answerable
only to the Secretary of State.

His fluency in Gaelic was not unique in the 19th-century

Scottish civil service. But a combination of his seniority, his formidable family connections and his ability actually to converse with the Highland poor led to Malcolm MacNeill's being given a number of tasks to perform in the Gaidhealtachd. Although he stood firmly on the side of the emigrators in the Highland question – MacNeill helped to organise a Canadian resettlement scheme for crofters – he exercised those responsibilities with sensitivity and diligence.

All of those assets combined in February 1883 to make Malcolm MacNeill the obvious envoy for the Government of William Gladstone to the crofters of Glendale. The fact that Balfour, Harcourt and Gladstone chose at that time to send a negotiator rather than a battalion of infantry to Skye is telling.

The practical problems, which certainly exercised the mind of Lord Advocate John Blair Balfour, were obvious. Where, after all, were the 300 armed policemen requested by McHardy and Ivory to be found? Members of Scottish constabularies were not, in the early 1880s, routinely trained in the use of firearms. Sending more bobbies from the Lowlands into isolated Highland glens, this time carrying pistols and rifles, was freighted with such obvious hazard that no chief constable outside Inverness-shire was likely to countenance the notion. Despatching troops might guarantee a more disciplined use of firepower but it also carried the obvious implications of British soldiers with guns being deployed against British citizens with sticks a stone's throw from the British mainland, as well as the strong possibility of both civilian and redcoat blood being shed, neither of which scenarios was cheerfully anticipated by a Liberal Government. In October 1882 William Harcourt had written to his right-wing party colleague, and future prime minister, Archibald Primrose, 5th Earl of Rosebery, warning that the imposition of a military solution in Skye would be 'with a dour folk like the Scotch most dangerous. It will bring up the Land question in the Highlands in a form which the lairds will bitterly regret.'

On top of that, Home Secretary Harcourt was increasingly in agreement with his prime minister about where the root cause of the problem lay. 'It is the fault of the silly lairds,' Harcourt told his wife in January 1883, 'who have brought us to this.' Like William Gladstone, William Harcourt's sympathies lay with the crofting classes of the Highlands rather than with their lairds. 'I doubt whether there is anybody in the House who knows Skye better than I do,' Harcourt would tell the Commons two years later. 'I have spent my leisure time for nearly 20 years mostly upon its shores and its bays; and all I can say is, that I have a deep sympathy and regard – I might almost use stronger terms – for the people who inhabit them. They are a people distinguished remarkably . . . by a mildness of character which seems to belong to the climate in which they live. They have a high-bred courtesy in their demeanour; they have a kindliness towards all who have dealings with them that is singularly attractive.'

In public, then, the British Government was happy to agree with the Inverness-shire authorities and the Edinburgh law lords that the laws of the land had been both flouted and broken by a lot of the people of the island of Skye, some of whom had even committed violent assault not only on estate shepherds but also on court messengers and police officers.

In private, the Government remained for the moment unconvinced that sending armed policemen or soldiers to the island would resolve rather than exacerbate the problem. More crucially, most senior members of the Government believed that the lawbreakers in Skye had broken the law for very good reasons, if not in extenuating circumstances.

Early in February 1883 Malcolm MacNeill travelled to the port of Rothesay on the island of Bute at the mouth of the River Clyde. There he boarded HMS *Jackal*, a 40-year-old hybrid vessel, half paddle steamer and half schooner. The *Jackal* had in her younger days seen service with her three small guns in the Mediterranean but since 1864 had been acting in dignified semi-retirement as a fishery protection vessel off the west coast of Scotland, where her two masts, stove-pipe funnel and modest 140–foot silhouette were a familiar sight.

The *Jackal* weighed anchor in Rothesay in the evening of Monday, 5 February 1883 with 'neither military nor police force on board'. She ploughed northwards through rough weather to Skye and – her experienced captain ignoring the fears of Sheriff-Substitute Peter Speirs that the loch could be mined – anchored in Loch Pooltiel very early in the morning of Friday, 9 February. A naval officer then went ashore at Glendale and was 'courteously' received by some Glendale crofters. The crofters' courtesy may have been partly because, as local oral recollection has it, 'the naval officer had borrowed a coat to hide his uniform "so as not to alarm locals".' It was also because the crofters of Glendale and elsewhere had, as they would later prove in more dangerous circumstances, enormous respect for the armed forces. It was agreed between the officer and the crofters that a meeting would be held in Glendale Free Church of Scotland at 2 p.m. that afternoon.

Once again the horns were blown from hilltops across Glendale, and by 2 p.m. 700 people had gathered in and around the small church, which was 'filled to an extent that was never before witnessed'. Malcolm MacNeill was accompanied into the assembly by Captain Allan MacDonald, another elderly scion of a Sleat tacksman who had become the landowner of Waternish in the north of Skye, and who had hurriedly been summoned from Waternish House, and by the local Free Church minister Reverend John MacRae.

MacNeill, MacDonald and MacRae were all Gaelic speakers and the proceedings which followed were largely conducted in that language. But they began with a prepared statement in English which was read aloud by Malcolm MacNeill and simultaneously translated into Gaelic by Reverend MacRae.

'Inhabitants of Glendale,' said Malcolm MacNeill, 'I have come here to speak to you one last word on behalf of the Government. It may be that you are not aware how serious is the offence which you have committed in deforcing and maltreating an officer carrying out the orders of the Supreme Court. If so, it is my duty to tell you that it is an offence which will neither be forgotten nor forgiven till four offenders, viz., John Macpherson, Malcolm Matheson, Donald Macleod, and John Morrison have surrendered themselves to receive the punishment they deserve.

'But whatever may have been your mistake on this point, every one of you is aware that to seize grazings belonging to another, to drive off his stock and servants without any legal authority whatever, is a gross breach of the law, even if you have a moral right to these grazings, a fact which must be clearly proved before it is admitted. Then, again, nothing can excuse organised assemblages for the express purpose of intimidation, if not of violence.

'Having now shortly described to you what are your offences, I have further to inform you that the Government are resolved to enforce law and order in Skye at whatever cost. No one need fear that injustice will be done him; but you seem to forget that justice, while she carries a balance in one hand, carries a sword in the other, and that however important may be her duties in removing grievances, those in punishing offenders are still more important.

'Some who call themselves your friends may tell you that you have only to resist to gain what you desire. It is my duty to warn you against such evil counsel. Your resistance to the law, and your riotous proceedings, are turning against you those who most earnestly desire to see your just claims satisfied. They begin to fear that your claims may turn out to be as bad as your behaviour has been.

'You will, perhaps, allow me to give you a word of advice. Let the men named, viz., John Macpherson, Malcolm Matheson, Donald Macleod, and John Morrison surrender themselves on board the *Jackal*. Let the stock be instantly removed in my presence from Waterstein. Let an intimation, signed for you by your elders, be sent to the tenant, promising security for his stock and servants. I shall now leave you to discuss this matter among yourselves, and I shall be here again to receive your answer on the 10th [Saturday, the following day], at ten o'clock.

'Meanwhile I should like to visit you in your houses, and to hear from your own mouth what are the grievances of which you complain. I trust you may arrive at a reasonable decision. If you persevere in your present attitude, though I shall regret what may befall you, I shall be obliged to admit that you have none to blame but yourselves.'

Captain Allan MacDonald then elaborated on the identity and motives of 'some who call themselves your friends'. MacDonald 'accused the crofters', reported the *Glasgow Herald*'s man at the scene, 'of attending to the advice of Irish Roman Catholics and disregarding that of their own clergymen and their own countrymen. Irish agitators told them that the more they contravened the law the more likely they were to have their grievances redressed, and the crofters had been giving effect to this foolish counsel.'

John MacPherson, who would be remembered in the following century by an elderly former neighbour as a 'duine dèanta dìreach, feusag gheal gu bhroilleach, agus teanga a sgoilteadh an darach' (a 'powerful man, a white beard down to his chest, and a tongue that could cleave oak'), replied from the front of the gathering. MacPherson 'repudiated these statements, and said that the proprietors were the cause of the agitation, as they had refused the crofters Waterstein, although a rent was offered for it. No-one had come from Ireland to give them advice and Mr McHugh was not paid any attention to.'

MacPherson insisted, reported Alexander MacKenzie of the *Celtic Magazine* 'that none of the people ever put cattle or sheep on Waterstein. The place was not fenced in, and it was perfectly impossible for the crofters to prevent their cattle from straying there.

'He then related how that eighteen years ago Tormore gave grazings for 150 sheep belonging to other tenants than those of Glendale; how, when the Milovaig people were away at the fishing, the shepherds put these sheep on their (the Milovaig tenants') land; how they were never taken off; and how, since they were deprived of grazing for 150 sheep for eighteen years, they were entitled to get something in return. They complained to Tormore of the giving of their grazing to other townships, but got no redress. They told the shepherds to take away these sheep to their own lands, but the shepherds, acting under Tormore's orders, would not.

'Captain Macdonald, of Waternish, said, if he (Macpherson) would go to Edinburgh, all this would be heard; they would be allowed to produce witnesses.'

John MacPherson continued relentlessly. He 'said the Milovaig tenants had been there for 37 years. When Tormore took Waterstein a year or so ago, he came there as a new tenant. Now, before Tormore, then factor, took Waterstein to himself, the crofters offered to take it at the old rent. They would not get it although they had been 37 years in the place. When Waterstein was out, was it not as fair for the crofters, so long there, to get it at the full rent, as it was for Tormore, the factor, to take it? Would the Government support them, and send witnesses after them to Edinburgh to prove this?

'Captain Macdonald said that any witnesses that would be cited by the Government would be paid. He had heard that Tormore offered to put up a march between his farm and the crofters' townships, but that the crofters would not allow him.

'John Macpherson said that was not correct. He had been 37 years in Milovaig, and he and the other crofters thought that no fence ought to have been put up without their having been consulted; the factor's fence was to have taken a straight line, and this would have taken some of the crofters' land away.' MacPherson 'denied that the shepherds had been maltreated on a recent occasion. They had just been remonstrated with and driven off the hill.'

The shopkeeper and postmaster Peter MacKinnon cited

his own Crimean War service as evidence of his loyalty to his country. 'He had been in Glendale for the last twenty years,' he said. 'He used at one time to buy the fish from the fishermen, but Tormore, when he came, would not allow him to do so; and by that act of tyranny, he had lost £100. He charged the factor's servants with having with their dogs driven his cow against a fence. The cow died, and he lost £12. He got no compensation for that.

'The Glendale people were never allowed to go to law, by the tyranny of the factor. Tormore was the Sheriff in this place. When he (Mackinnon) went to Tormore, and bitterly complained of his conduct in preventing the fishermen from selling their fish to him, and in taking the fish himself, Tormore's answer was, "You are reading too many newspapers, and you don't deserve to get justice."

'During the time of his factorship Tormore never allowed any case in dispute to go before the Sheriff at Portree, but he decided them in his own way. The people would be evicted if they went against his decision. What the people now wanted to do was to break this tyranny of factors and proprietors, and not to break the law.

'For 20 years there had been no law in Glendale, but the law of the factor ... The present factor was as bad as the other. Solomon, that was Tormore, beat them with swords;' said MacKinnon, raising a cheer from the assembled crofters, 'but Rehoboam, that was [John Robertson of] Greshornish, tormented them with scorpions.'

A crofter asked about rumours that the army was to be sent to Glendale. Captain Allan MacDonald replied that 'no soldiers had yet been sent ... but that if the offer of Mr MacNeill was not accepted there was every probability that the Government would vindicate the law by sending an armed force.'

Peter MacKinnon then declared that 'the men might find their way to the Court of Session, but the [other] conditions asked by Mr MacNeill would never be consented to. The sun and the moon would change their course before they would agree to the conditions stipulated.'

Just as the meeting broke up, a crofter 'said that matters would never be settled in Glendale until a Royal Commission was granted or concessions were made by the proprietors'.

Reverend John MacRae then called a further meeting with his flock of recalcitrant crofters. At that gathering the Dunvegan merchant Peter MacLean pointed out that 'it was pretty evident that the four men would be arrested if they did not now surrender. This would bring an armed force into the district, a thing which was not at all desirable'. MacLean advised 'that they should comply with the first condition in the Government statement, assuring the men that their wives and families would be looked after in their absence. He also counselled them not to compromise themselves by any written statements.'

As it happened, only three of the four wanted crofters were in Glendale that day. John MacPherson, Donald MacLeod and John Morrison were there, but Malcolm Matheson was away in the island of Lewis training for the Royal Naval Reserve. MacPherson, MacLeod and Morrison agreed to travel to the Court of Session in Edinburgh. A show of hands was then requested from their fellow crofters, 'and there was a unanimous vote in favour of surrender'.

It was very far from an unconditional surrender. On Saturday morning Peter MacKinnon received at his post office a letter from Malcolm MacNeill aboard the *Jackal* in Loch Pooltiel. MacNeill, who was anxious not to return empty-handed, asked MacKinnon to make it doubly clear that 'the only offence the crofters were charged with on this occasion was with failing to obey the Court of Session by appearing at the bar'. MacNeill added that he personally would be happy to contribute to a fund to assist other crofters to travel as witnesses to Edinburgh if and when they were required. The *Jackal* would leave at 1 p.m., said MacNeill, and he would like to know before that hour what the men intended to do.

Later in the morning MacNeill received his answer. The Glendale crofters would go to the Court of Session in Edinburgh. But they would not remove any 'stray' stock from Waterstein and they would not send any written guarantees of 'security' to factor John Robertson.

They would not, for that matter, subject themselves to the indignity of travelling south on the *Jackal*. Instead they would board the civilian passenger ship MV *Dunara Castle* at Dunvegan on Monday morning – in the words of John MacPherson this would 'look better, and besides, they would have their liberty'. They would not have it said of them by future generations of their countrymen, insisted MacPherson, 'that Glendale men had to be taken away from their homes in a man-of-war'.

Having had terms dictated to him, Malcolm MacNeill left Loch Pooltiel and returned to the south. Two days later, on the morning of Monday, 12 February, John MacPherson, Donald MacLeod and John Morrison boarded the *Dunara Castle* at Dunvegan 'after bidding farewell to their families and friends, many of whom were steeped in tears'.

'John Macpherson,' reported the *Inverness Courier*, 'who is a man of striking appearance, bold and manly bearing, great intelligence, and considerable mental power, had a word of comfort and re-assurance for all. "If I was going," he said to them in Gaelic, "to jail for a sheep or for a lamb, you might be very sorry. But, as it is, you ought to be very glad. For we go to uphold a good cause; we go to defend the widow and the fatherless, and the comfort and needs of our hearths and homes."

'This he told to his wife and family, and, with these characteristic words, delivered with the eloquence for which he is distinguished among his fellows, he reassured the people who gathered here and there on the roadside between Milovaig and Colbost.'

The crofters who remained behind in Glendale, reported the *Glasgow Herald*, 'think there is a chance of their [four neighbours] being pardoned. They also think the sending of the gunboat by the Government may be a preliminary step before a

Royal Commission is promised.' Those crofters were half right.

By February 1883 the curious eyes of the whole of the United Kingdom were on Glendale. The meetings in Glendale Free Church and the subsequent passage of the three men from Skye to Edinburgh were sympathetically reported not only in Scotland and London, but also as far afield as Chelmsford, Tamworth and Exeter in the English shires. Their supporters were then given a boost from an unexpected source.

MacPherson, MacLeod and Morrison arrived in Glasgow on Wednesday the 14th. They were met by friends and well-wishers who accommodated them in a hotel. The Court of Session in Edinburgh was then informed by letter that their suspects were in the Lowlands and awaiting notification of a trial date.

The contents of that letter inevitably made their way to messenger-at-arms Donald MacTavish at his Glasgow home. Equally inevitably, MacTavish seized the opportunity for revenge. It backfired horribly.

Shortly before 6 a.m., at least two hours before daybreak on Friday, 16 February, Donald MacTavish burst into the Glendale men's hotel room, arrested them and refused them breakfast before hurrying them by train from Glasgow to Calton Prison in Edinburgh. At Calton Prison, however, the governor refused to admit MacPherson, MacLeod and Morrison on the grounds that Donald MacTavish's arrest warrant was insufficient reason for imprisonment. The messenger-at-arms was therefore obliged to book them at the expense of his employers into an Edinburgh hotel, where he detained them under informal house arrest until they were finally called to the bar of the Court of Session on Tuesday, 20 February.

In the House of Commons, Donald Macfarlane, Dr Charles Cameron and Charles Fraser Mackintosh made hay. 'I wish to ask the Lord Advocate a Question,' said Macfarlane to John Blair Balfour, 'of which I have given him private Notice. It is, if he can state whether it is a fact that the three men who were proceeding from Skye to Edinburgh have been arrested in Glasgow, by whom they were arrested, and for what reason was their arrest necessary, as they were voluntarily surrendering themselves to the law? And I wish further to ask the right hon. and learned Gentleman, with reference to the answer on Friday that only three men had surrendered, whether it is a fact or not that the fourth man has not surrendered because he was on duty as a Coastguardsman?'

With reference to the Glendale crofters arrested in Glasgow on Friday, Cameron asked 'whether the private parties at whose instance they were arrested communicated with the Crown authorities before taking them into custody; whether the prison authorities at Edinburgh, to which city they were conveyed, refused to accept their custody; whether they were thereupon lodged in the Ship Hotel, Edinburgh, and confined there for several days in charge of the messenger-at-arms who apprehended them; and, under what Law it is competent thus privately to confine prisoners, civil or criminal, for days together, in a city containing a public prison?'

Charles Fraser Mackintosh wished to know 'What steps Government intend to take in consequence of the apprehension, on their journey to Edinburgh, of three Glendale crofters, in their beds in Glasgow, at six o'clock in the morning of Friday, 16th February, in face of the promise (accepted by the special Government Commissioner to Skye) of these crofters to attend before the Supreme Court of Scotland?'

Balfour was courteously helpless. The fourth wanted man, he told Macfarlane, was not a Coastguardsman but was 'serving somewhere in the Naval Reserve, but I have no official information on that matter'. As for the arrest of the other three, it had been done 'at the instance of the private parties who were petitioners in the Petition for breach of interdict, under the warrant which the Court gave for their arrest . . . The arrest has not been by the Government . . . as the men are in the hands of competent advisers, I do not feel called upon to offer any opinion as to its legality'.

When they did appear in court MacPherson, MacLeod and Morrison were immediately granted bail of £100 each. The sums were guaranteed by three eminent Edinburgh Highlanders, and the hearings got underway through a Gaelic interpreter before Lord Shand and a packed audience of supporters and reporters.

John MacPherson would always thereafter insist that the defendants' case was both legally and morally watertight. It was undeniable that Milovaig stock had found its way onto Waterstein. But the absence, for whatever reason, of a permanent dyke or fence could not be blamed on any crofter, let alone on the four men who were on trial in Edinburgh. Sheep and cattle could not be expected to obey interdicts.

Moreover, the absence of fences cut both ways. 'The order of the Court,' reported Alexander MacKenzie, 'was to prevent the people of Milovaig doing on Waterstein what the Waterstein people were doing on Milovaig; and, considering all the circumstances, that would necessarily create irritation. There was only general evidence that sheep came upon Waterstein, and were driven back on the Milovaig townships.

'In his evidence [John] Macpherson said that the sheep might have been backwards and forwards over the marches, and as there were no fences, and as the work had to be done by shepherds, that was a thing which could not have been prevented . . . The second point against them was that they trespassed on the lands of Waterstein without any valid excuse. Now, if anyone went on Waterstein for an illegal purpose, that would be trespass; but if they went to speak to the shepherds on business in a friendly way, the element of trespass would not enter.'

'To speak to the shepherds on business in a friendly way.' In alleged instances of intimidation or assault it proved difficult for almost all of the offended parties to identify any single crofter as having been present, let alone guilty of the offence. John MacPherson in particular was elusive, having hardly ever been spotted on Waterstein except on those occasions when he might have been innocently rounding up his own stray stock for return to their Milovaig grazings, or debating with shepherds the best way to keep their herds apart.

The legal fallibility of the defence was, however, straight-forward. No interdict had ever been sought or gained by the crofters to prevent Waterstein stock from grazing on Milovaig land. But interdicts had been sought, and gained on numerous occasions, by the MacPherson estate to stop Milovaig stock fattening itself on Waterstein turf.

That was the essential point at issue. Other matters of who did what else and when, and of ancient traditional rights, were not before the court. The crofters' moral high ground was under-mined by the evidence given in Gaelic by two former Waterstein shepherds. Seventy-year-old John MacDermid testified that 'a number of crofters' had gone to his door and told him that unless he stopped turning Milovaig cattle off Waterstein they would 'throw down the house . . . They had made others cease, and would make him cease too'.

The other retired shepherd bore the common name of Donald MacDonald. 'A few days after Martinmas,' testified MacDonald, as reported by the *Edinburgh Evening News*, 'when he was driving some sheep onto the Milovaig ground and as he was coming along the road towards Ramasig, he met a number of the men, among whom was [the Naval Reservist Malcolm] Mathieson. Witness was struck twice by someone whom he did not know. They told him they would drive him off the ground altogether. One of them got a hold of witness by the back of his coat, and dragged him backwards. The Miloveig men drove witness in front of them all the way from Ramasig to Hamara, a distance . . . of about four miles . . . He left Waterstein that day . . .'

Donald MacDonald may not have been able or willing to identify all of his assailants, but his fellow shepherd Donald Nicholson, who had also been present, named them in court as 'John Morrison, Malcolm Mathieson, Archibald Gillies, Donald MacLeod, John Macpherson, Neil Macpherson and

Alan MacKinnon'. Four of those six names were presently on trial, although Malcolm Matheson was still being tried in absentia.

Alexander Burns Shand, Lord Shand, was a native of Aberdeen who had been raised in Glasgow. He had been a Lord of Session for the past 11 years and had stood at the Scottish Bar since 1853. He was a political liberal with a particular interest in the responsibility of employers for the health and safety of their employees. Whether or not that inclined Lord Shand to sympathy with the unsafe employed shepherds of Waterstein, he found little difficulty in reaching a verdict on the four crofters from Glendale.

In giving judgement, Lord Shand stressed that just one 'single question' had been raised by the proceedings in this case. It was 'whether the respondents have committed a breach of the interdict or order of this Court.

'That interdict,' he continued, 'was granted upon the 6th July, 1882, and was duly intimated to the respondents and a number of other crofters in Milovaig, as the original interdict had also been duly intimated to them. The order of the Court was an interdict, as has been pointed out by the complainer's counsel, striking at three different acts on the part of the respondents.

'The Court interdicted, and prohibited, and discharged the respondents entering or trespassing upon the lands or farm of Waterstein. Again, they were interdicted from pasturing or herding their sheep or cattle on those lands or any part thereof, and from allowing their sheep, horses, or cattle, to stray thereon, or on part thereon; and, finally, they were interdicted from obstructing, molesting, or interfering with the complainers in the occupation of the lands or farm, or with their tenants, dependants, or servants.

'I regret to say that I have come to the conclusion, and come to the conclusion without the smallest difficulty, that the respondents have each and all of them been guilty of a violation of the order of the Court.'

They were guilty of Contempt of Court. It was not a verdict which any reasonable person could contradict. Virtually everybody in Glendale had in recent times made their contempt of court orders perfectly obvious. But the men had travelled to Edinburgh with the expectation of receiving natural justice rather than statutory justice. They had anticipated that their mere appearance at the Court of Session would mollify the authorities. They had hoped to be granted a national platform upon which to air their grievances. Alexander Burns Shand could not and did not see proceedings in his Court of Session in the same light.

His sentences were, he said, influenced by the fact that contempt of court orders in Glendale had been 'in some instances, accompanied by serious violence' against estate shepherds. None of the men was on trial for injuriously driving police officers and messengers-at-arms out of their district, and nobody ever would be prosecuted for those offences. But Lord Shand was not a hermit; he and his fellow law lords knew perfectly well what had happened to the six policemen and to Donald MacTavish and James MacRaild in Glendale on the 16th and 17th January 1883.

Each one of the four men from Lower Milovaig, the 48–year-old John MacPherson, the 22–year-old Donald MacLeod, the 59–year-old John Morrison and in his absence the 37–year-old Malcolm Matheson, were sentenced to two months' imprisonment.

The court gasped and muttered. Then, as the three men were led from the dock, the crowded public benches rose to applaud them.

They were taken by cab to Calton Prison, where this time the governor admitted them. Initially their treatment was unreasonably harsh. They were dressed in prisoners' drabs, put in cells to sleep on hard wooden boards and told that their hair must be shorn. MacLeod and Morrison were duly close-shaven. John MacPherson somehow managed to talk his way out of the barber's grasp until the following day. That reprieve was enough. Their legal representation arrived and pointed out to the governor of Calton Prison that his new charges were not 'common criminals' and that the comparatively mild, civil nature of their offences allowed them 'to be treated in quite a different manner'.

Alexander MacKenzie, who visited them in prison, wrote afterwards, 'The officials could not replace the hair so unwarrantably cut off on the previous evening, but to the men's great satisfaction their own clothes was returned to them next morning. They were told that, according to the regulations, friends would be permitted to visit them; that they might receive food from outside, if they, or their friends, chose to supply and pay for it; that they could have any books and newspapers supplied to them, at their own expense or at that of their friends; and that they were to take their exercise separately from the criminals in the prison.

'Instead of the hard boards, as they had for the first night, to sleep on, they were supplied with excellent beds and bedding; they were placed together in a large room, and amply provided with fire, and other conveniences; while the only work of any kind they had to perform, was to scrub out their own room twice a week; and this the regulations permitted them to get done by others, if they preferred to pay for it.

'Their food was supplied daily, three times a day, from a neighbouring restaurant, by the Edinburgh Highland Land Law Reform Association, through Mr. Dugald Cowan, Secretary, who also supplied them with books, magazines, and newspapers, and such other little comforts as the prison regulations admitted of . . .

'They expressed themselves extremely grateful for the interest taken by outsiders in their case, and in their families, and desired us to intimate to their friends that they were more comfortable in prison than they could possibly have expected; that every official was as considerate as the regulations would allow; and that they had nothing but good to say of everyone connected with the prison. We found them all in the same room, provided with the best bedding and a good fire.

'They strongly urged that their friends at home should not commit any act which would bring odium on those who sympathised with them outside, and that they should keep strictly within the law. John Morrison, the eldest of the three had been complaining, but he was fast recovering, and the others were in excellent health and spirits.

'Believing that the circumstance was not accidental, they were much delighted at the enlivenment of their evenings by frequently hearing the bagpipes, in the neighbourhood, playing familiar airs, an arrangement by their Edinburgh friends of a remarkably considerate and delicate nature. The only thing they complained of was that John Macpherson, the only one of the three who could write, had been deprived of writing materials. Otherwise, they were as happy and comfortable as people within a prison, deprived of their liberty, could possibly be. But they were much concerned about their families, and afraid that their crofts might suffer from want of the necessary cultivation and attention to the other Spring work, during their imprisonment.'

Back in Skye the word of the convictions and sentences was received with 'great surprise and deep sorrow. When the news reached Glendale the people would not give credence to it at first, as they were under the impression, after perusing the account of the trial in the newspapers, that the prosecution had failed in proving the averments; but, on learning beyond doubt that the crofters were sentenced to two months' imprisonment, their feelings of incredulity gave way to that of indignation, which is entirely directed against the trustees of the estate, as they attribute the whole disturbance to to the unyielding attitude and unconciliatory treatment of the trustees towards the tenants.

'The people now freely state,' a correspondent telegraphed from Dunvegan to the *Dundee Evening Telegraph*, 'that they will carry on the agitation to the bitter end, and will never surrender until their grievances are redressed. The sentence of the Court of Session has tended to cause the agitation to spread and take a deeper root and hold on the minds of the people.'

That agitation was eased by a significant intervention 650 miles to the south of Glendale. On 19 March 1883 Donald Macfarlane MP rose in the House of Commons to ask the Home Secretary, William Harcourt, 'If his attention has been called to the sentence passed upon the three Glendale Crofters who had voluntarily surrendered themselves to answer the charge made against them; and, if, in consideration of the fact of their voluntary surrender, and that their offence arose more from ignorance than deliberate resistance to the Law, he will remit the whole, or at least a portion, of the sentence of two months' imprisonment to which they have been sentenced?'

'This being contempt of the orders of a Court,' replied Harcourt, 'I have no authority to remit the sentence. I do not wish, however, to rest upon that alone. If I had such authority, I should not think it right to interfere with a sentence pronounced by a Court to vindicate the law from what was pronounced to be a deliberate and organized combination to resist the law.'

He then delivered his trump. 'I may, perhaps,' said the Home Secretary, 'be allowed to state what I have been frequently asked, and could not answer.

'The Royal Commission to inquire into the condition of the crofters and cottars has now been sanctioned by Her Majesty; and, with the permission of the House, I will mention the names of the Commissioners. The Chairman will be Lord Napier and Ettrick; and the other Members will be Sir Kenneth Mackenzie, of Gairloch; Mr. Donald Cameron, of Lochiel; Mr. C.F. Mackintosh, M.P.; Sheriff Nicolson, of Kirkcudbright, and Professor MacKinnon.

'Mr. Malcolm McNeill, who recently visited Skye for the purpose of inquiring into the question, will be the Secretary. The terms of the Commission will be – "To inquire into the condition of the crofters and cottars in the Highlands and Islands of Scotland, and all matters affecting the same or relating thereto, and to report thereon."'

The Commission of Inquiry which had been dismissed by both Prime Minister William Gladstone and Lord Advocate Balfour as recently as November 1882, was three months later established, staffed and ready to go. It had of course been agreed by Gladstone, Harcourt and Balfour many weeks earlier. Malcolm MacNeill knew and whispered about it during his visit to Glendale on the *Jackal*. The presence of Charles Fraser Mackintosh as well as MacNeill on the Commission guaranteed that Mackintosh's Inverness friends and allies such as Alexander MacKenzie and John Murdoch knew of the imminent announcement.

All it had required was the sacrificial imprisonment of a few men from Glendale, so that the Liberal Government was not vulnerable to charges from landowning interests of favouring the claims of militant crofters against the maintenance of the law.

Harcourt's announcement had the desired response. The people of Glendale continued their rent strike and muttered that they might not hand over Malcolm Matheson to do his two-month stretch in Calton Prison. But they also drove all of their stock off Waterstein, announced their decision to put in another legal bid to rent the farm, and sat back and waited for the Royal Commission to arrive.

They did not have to wait for long. The body which would become known as the Napier Commission acted with remarkable speed. Having been unveiled by William Harcourt in the House of Commons on Monday, 19 March 1883, it held its first hearing just seven weeks later, in Braes in Skye on Tuesday, 8 May.

That brief interregnum left time for two developments. With John MacPherson, Donald MacLeod and John Morrison still in Calton Prison, with Lord Napier and his colleagues packing their bags and preparing to sail to the north-west Highlands and

Islands, on 6 April the agents and trustees of the Glendale estate decided to mount a decisive assault on the rent strike by issuing almost 70 notices of eviction which, had they been carried out, would have emptied the village of Lower Milovaig and picked off troublemakers elsewhere throughout Glendale. Altogether, some 400 men, women and children would have been made homeless by the evictions. 'The landlord party in Glendale,' reported the *Dundee Evening Telegraph*, 'are determined to exercise their legal rights to the utmost limit, and if the evictions are insisted upon it is almost certain that a violent collision with the legal executive will take place, a collision, too, in which the Glendale men will be joined by numerous volunteers from all parts of Skye.'

The notices were taken out in Portree and entrusted to the local sheriff officer, Angus 'Dubh' MacLeod. Once again, Angus Dubh got no further than Skinidin, where on 10 April he was met on the narrow road by a crowd of 1,000 people. 'Angus,' reported Alexander MacKenzie, 'realising the position of affairs, and feeling that discretion was the better part of valour, decided to act upon the maxim that "he who fights and runs away may live to fight another day", at once turned right about, and made off at full speed to Dunvegan, from whence, the same afternoon, he despatched the summonses to the Law-agent of the proprietors, at Portree, intimating that he would not, on any account, make a further attempt to serve them.

'The people were thoroughly determined not to accept service, and they made arrangements by which notice was to be given to the whole of Skye, to come to their aid, by the lighting of fires at night, or exhibiting flags by day, on certain hills throughout the island, which could be seen the one from the other, thus intimating the approach of a police or military force in a few minutes to the whole island, the population of which, it is now no secret, almost to a man, had intimated their determination to come to the rescue of the people of Glendale in the event of their aid being required.'

The eviction notices were never served by hand. Instead, they were posted from Portree by registered letter. Peter MacKinnon, being the Glendale postmaster, was obliged to open his, and proceeded to ignore it. The others were never even collected. In the House of Commons on 16 April, Donald Macfarlane asked William Harcourt, 'If his attention has been called to a statement in the newspapers, that seventy Glendale Crofters have been served, or are about to be served, with notices of eviction; and, if this statement is correct, whether he proposes to take any steps to prevent the removal of the people pending an inquiry into their case by the Royal Commission?'

Harcourt drew a deep breath. 'I have no knowledge of the details to which the first part of the Question of the hon. Member alludes;' he said, 'and with regard to the second part, the hon. Gentleman must be aware that I have no power to suspend the operations of the law.

'It would, moreover, be a very bad thing if we thought that the appointment of an impartial inquiry should offer any justification or excuse for the non-observance of the law. On the contrary, the existence of such an inquiry ought rather to encourage people to be patient, and to observe the law.'

The Napier Commission was scheduled to take evidence in Glendale Free Church on Saturday, 19 May 1883. Four days earlier, at 8 a.m. on 15 May John MacPherson, Donald MacLeod and John Morrison were released from Calton Prison. They were met at the prison doors by 'about 1,000 people, headed by two pipers, who marched to the Ship Hotel, and there entertained the liberated men to a public breakfast.

'The same evening John Macpherson, after visiting his friends in Glasgow, proceeded to Skye, by Strome Ferry, that he might reach Glendale in time to be examined by the Royal Commission on the following Saturday. It became known in Skye that he was coming, and the Portree and Braes people determined to give him a hearty reception. As the *Clydesdale* approached the Braes, three bonfires were noticed ablaze, and several flags were flying aloft, in the distance.'

On the evening of Thursday, 17 May John MacPherson set foot once again in Skye. 'When the steamer rounded into Portree Bay, a large crowd congregated on the pier, while numbers were flocking from all parts of the village in the same direction. Macpherson having been observed on deck, the crowd cheered vociferously, while hats were raised and handkerchiefs waved by the assembled multitude.

'Before he could place his foot on shore he was raised on the shoulders of four stalwart fellows, who carried him aloft, hat in hand, bowing to the crowd, amid the enthusiasm of the people, to the Portree Hotel, a piper leading the way, playing appropriate airs. Macpherson, on his arrival at the hotel, addressed the people, warmly thanking all his friends and the friends of the people of Skye, north and south, and urging upon his countrymen to insist upon getting justice now that it was within their reach.'

John MacPherson mounted an empty beer cask placed outside the Portree Hotel, the better to reach out to the multitude gathered in the village square.

'"If Joseph," he said, "had never been sent into Egyptian bondage, the children of Israel might never have got out of it." He believed the imprisonment of the Glendale crofters had done more to remove landlord tyranny and oppression from Skye than anything which happened during the present century. He was afterwards entertained in the hotel by many of the leading inhabitants of Portree, where several of the Braes men came all the way to pay honour, on his return from prison, to one whom they esteemed as the leading martyr in the crofter cause.'

That was the first time on public record that any one of the Glendale men, or any other campaigner in Skye, was referred to as a 'martyr'. The word stuck. John MacPherson spent that Thursday night in Portree and on Friday he returned to Lower Milovaig.

John MacPherson's appearance before the Napier Commission in Glendale on the morning of Saturday, 19 May, could have been choreographed, and probably was. The commissioners had been put ashore from Loch Pooltiel at Meanish jetty. From there they were obliged to walk past Lower and Upper Milovaig to Glendale Free Church. 'When I spoke with the late Neil MacLean from Milovaig in 1981,' said Allan Campbell of Colbost, 'he told how the crofters prepared a special welcome for the Commission. When the Commission members rounded the corner at Hamara they were confronted by a banner made from old flour sacks and red cloth suspended above the road – it read "Down with landlords!"'

Once inside the Free Church, John MacPherson knew by sight three, and possibly four, of the seven men before him. The Commission's secretary, Malcolm MacNeill, was of course familiar to him following MacNeill's visit to Glendale in February. Among the six commissioners was Donald MacKinnon of Colonsay, who had recently become the first professor of Celtic at Edinburgh University, and who had acted as official interpreter at the trial of MacPherson, Donald MacLeod, John Morrison and Malcolm Matheson in the Court of Session nine weeks earlier. There was also Charles Fraser Mackintosh, the supportive Liberal MP for Inverness Burghs.

If John MacPherson did not personally know, he would have known of Sheriff Alexander Nicolson, not least through his fellow Skyeman's Glendale boyhood and his anti-Land League pamphleteering a year earlier. The other two Highlanders represented the major landowning interest. One, Sir Kenneth MacKenzie of Gairloch, had the reputation of a paternalist landowner. MacKenzie had stood for the Liberal Party in Inverness-shire in the general election of 1880, but had been beaten by the Conservative candidate, his fellow commissioner Donald Cameron of Lochiel. Cameron was therefore the sitting Tory Member of Parliament for Skye and the rest of rural Inverness-shire.

The chair, Francis, 10th Lord Napier, was of a celebrated and accomplished Borders family. At 64 years old Napier himself was at the end of a diplomatic career which had reached its peak when he served as Governor of Madras between 1866 and 1872 and then as acting Viceroy of India for four months early in 1872. A few years earlier the *New York Times* had described Napier as 'considerably above middle size, strong, healthy, with calm, handsome face, gray hair and whiskers, an early riser, very often a late goer to bed, gifted with inexhaustible energy, tact, common sense and acuteness of judgement'.

John MacPherson looked straight at that 'calm, handsome face' on the morning of Saturday, 19 May 1883, and said: 'I would wish, my Lord and Gentlemen, that I would not be blamed for telling the truth – that no hurt would be done to me – for I got sixty-one days' imprisonment already for telling the truth, and asking for justice.'

'Do you ask for an assurance on our part?' asked Lord Napier. 'We are not able to give you any such assurance. It must be explained to you that the Commission cannot interfere in any respect between you and your landlord, or between you and the law, in case you should fall under the law; but we understand that no molestation will be offered by the landlord or by any one here on account of what occurs today.'

John MacPherson remained silent. John Robertson, the estate factor, had a hurried conversation with the estate trustee at his side, Reverend Hugh MacPherson, and then announced, 'On the part of the trustees of this property, I beg to say that no interference whatever will be made with John MacPherson or any other witness here, for giving such evidence as they think proper.'

Before he had answered a single question, John MacPherson had made his point. He proceeded to read a statement on behalf of his fellow crofters in Lower Milovaig, repeating their desire for Waterstein and their maltreatment by successive factors.

'We now state the demands of the crofters,' the statement concluded, '(a) The right to buy our holdings for so many years' rent, and to have them increased to as much land as will support a family in comfort; (b) That we shall not be removed from our holdings as long as we pay fair rents; (c) That that rent be fixed by a land court; (d) That we shall have compensation for whatever improvements on our dwelling-houses and crofts, in the event of our being removed; and (e) The power to buy our lands after paying our rents for so many years to Government.'

John MacPherson was cross-questioned for the rest of that Saturday and was briefly recalled when the Commission reconvened on the morning of Monday, 21 May. He had been given the national audience which he had largely been denied by the Court of Session in March. He was then followed by the representatives of other townships in Glendale, who repeated in Gaelic and in English the grievances and aspirations of their people. On the evening of 21 May the commissioners returned to their refitted quarters on a steamship in Loch Pooltiel and set off for their next appointment on the island of Raasay.

Between 8 May and 26 December 1883 the Napier Commission explored the whole of the north and west Highlands and Islands. They took evidence in St Kilda, 40 miles west of the Outer Hebrides, and at Baltasound in the north of the Shetland Islands, at Lybster in Caithness and at Bunessan in the island of Mull. The commissioners held meetings in 61 different places and heard from 775 people. Their transcripts, correspondence and recommendations were published in five volumes in April 1884. The volumes contained 500 pages of written submissions and 3,375 pages of oral evidence.

Lord Napier and his colleagues presented Parliament and the people of the United Kingdom with a first-hand history of the whole of the Highlands and Islands throughout the 19th century. It was not a pretty story. Not every crofter or landless cottar told the full truth. A tiny minority exaggerated and even invented complaints. But the commissioners' questioning – they asked 46,750 questions – was forensic and unflagging. Substantial time and space was given to large landowners, tacksmen and factors such as Donald 'Tormore' MacDonald to air their views and offer their counter-histories both in person and by written submission. Tormore and his associates seized the opportunity with relish, frequently returning in person to the Commission at different venues to put denials or accusations or character assassinations of their tenants and others on the public record. Nonetheless, by the end of 1883 the commissioners had, to the discomfort of at least a couple of their members, assembled a remarkably cogent and consistent narrative of irresponsible and abusive behaviour by landlords throughout the north and west of the country.

In Napier's own words, 'Many of the allegations of oppression and suffering with which these pages are painfully loaded would not bear a searching analysis. Under such a scrutiny they would be found erroneous as to time, to place, to persons, to extent, and misconstrued as to intention.

'It does not follow, however, that because these narratives are incorrect in detail, they are incorrect in colour or in kind. The history of the economical transformation which a great portion of the Highlands and Islands has during the past century undergone does not repose on the loose and legendary tales that pass from mouth to mouth; it rests on the solid basis of contemporary records, and if these were wanting, it is written in indelible characters on the surface of the soil.

'Changes of this nature, going to the very foundation of social and domestic life, are not anywhere accomplished without some constraint, resistance, and distress, and if the instances produced for our information are not specifically and literally true, they are akin to truth. In making these reservations and distinctions in regard to the accuracy of the evidence submitted to our notice, it is right to add that even among the poorest and least educated class who came before us there were many examples of candour, kindness, and native intelligence, testifying to the unaltered worth of the Highland people.'

Lord Napier and his colleagues had accidentally discovered that the evidence of landowning misbehaviour which was

offered in Glendale was far from unique. It was in fact typical
of almost every other part of Skye, every other island and every
other parish in what would become known as the crofting
counties. The Government-appointed investigation which was
triggered by the trial and imprisonment of three Glendale men
early in 1883 did exactly what had been expected of it by the
likes of John Murdoch, Alexander MacKenzie, Charles Fraser
Mackintosh and even John MacPherson. It opened Pandora's
box.

As a postscript to such an overwhelming body of evidence,
the recommendations of the commissioners were almost irrel-
evant. The six men were naturally divided. They all appended
their names to the timid joint statement that 'It may be that an
occasion is approaching for a partial redistribution of occupancy,
in which the extension of the crofting area will find a place. To
us it seems that the moment is favourable for the intervention
of legislation, by which an impulse may be given towards the
consolidation and enlargement of small holdings.'

This would be achieved chiefly by giving the traditional
Highland 'crofting township' – 'of which much has recently
been said and written, [but which] has never possessed any
corporate existence in the law of Scotland' – some legislative
legitimacy 'as a distinct agricultural area or unit, endowing it at
the same time with certain immunities and powers by which it
may attain stability, improvement, and expansion'.

But there could be no serious 'intervention' in the principle
of private property; 'a partial redistribution' of land should only
be encouraged by the Government when an unlikely consensus
existed between landlord and tenant, and even then only when a
crofting township was provenly overcrowded, in which case the
Government might offer grants to the landowner in return for
creating more crofting land.

The Commission rejected any notion of security of tenure for
all but the tenants of substantial acreages, which excluded most
crofters and all cottars. It rejected the proposal of an impartial

body to establish fair rents. It spoke favourably of the potential of orderly emigration schemes to North America and Australasia.

Any crofter who was paying £6 or more a year in rent, suggested Napier, should be given a 30–year lease as a fully paid-up member of one of his model crofting townships. Anybody who was paying less than £6 a year in rent should be helped on their way to Manitoba or New South Wales. The 20 crofters of Lower Milovaig, to take one pertinent and typical example, paid – or would have paid if they had not been on rent strike since 1882 – between £3 16s and £5 a year for the crofts which, within John MacPherson's lifetime, had been halved in size to accommodate refugees from elsewhere in north-western Skye. There would have been no place for MacPherson or any of his neighbours in Lord Napier's new Highlands.

Even then, the two major landholding commissioners dissented. Sir Kenneth MacKenzie of Gairloch set his face squarely against the extension – or even the existence – of crofting common grazings. Common grazings were essential to the character and existence of crofting. Sir Kenneth regarded them, and therefore crofting itself, as economically retrogressive and socially communistic in an era which should be considering instead the prospect of the Highlands and Islands 'dotted over' by small private farms 'occupied by a flourishing peasantry'.

Donald Cameron of Lochiel MP wanted the status quo, if not the status quo ante. His personal proposals bore a striking resemblance to the situation which had pertained in the Highlands for the previous century. There could not and should not, considered Lochiel, be any agent of change in the crofting counties other than the landowners. 'I would submit,' he wrote, 'that not only is the proprietor likely to be a better judge than any other authority as to whether a township is overcrowded, but he is in a far better position to form an opinion as to the chances of success in an attempt to increase the area of the township, or to relieve the congestion of the population by the removal of individual tenants to other suitable places on his property.'

'No one can have the same opportunities of ascertaining the inclinations of his crofters, their means or character. No one is better able to judge which of the crofters would be most capable of profitably occupying land which he might be in a position to offer them, while he alone possesses the requisite information to enable him to dispose satisfactorily of the crofts thus vacated . . .

'He might transplant half a dozen carefully selected industrious families to some vacant sheep farm, perhaps ten miles distant from their former homes, and redistribute their crofts among the most deserving of those that remain, thus giving encouragement and hope to all on his estate, that by industry and perseverance they may in their turn rise from the lamentable condition in which many of them now are to that of small but independent land-holding families . . .

'It is hardly necessary to point out,' said Cameron of Lochiel, 'that such a result can never be obtained through any compulsory Act of Parliament which the ingenuity of legislators can devise.' Cameron would later write to William Harcourt saying that not even Napier himself believed in the practicality of his own proposals. 'He [Napier] has told me privately,' said Cameron, 'not once, but often, that he knew his scheme has little chance of acceptance; that no Government could think of recommending to Parliament even the more innocent portions of it, and he gave me the impression that it was dream of a blessed and ideal condition of things that he wished to bring about, but knew he could not do . . .'

Lochiel's fellow Member of Parliament Charles Fraser Mackintosh also dissented, but for reasons opposed to those of Cameron of Lochiel. Fraser Mackintosh considered that Napier's recommendations denied the claims of such ordinary, small crofters as the people of Lower Milovaig. 'The fixing of £6 will cut out so many deserving crofters that I cannot be a party to their exclusion from the humane proposals in the Report,' he submitted. Although Fraser Mackintosh was prepared to accept an annual rental of £4 rather than £6 as the notional basement before exile, he preferred wholesale land reform. 'Re-occupation by, and re-distribution among, crofters and cottars of much land now used as large farms will be beneficial to the State, to the owner, and to the occupier,' he said.

The two Hebrideans in the pack, Professor Donald MacKinnon and Sheriff-Substitute Alexander Nicolson, were presumably in accord with Lord Napier. Crucially, however, Home Secretary William Harcourt was deeply unimpressed by any of them. Harcourt considered that Napier should have limited himself to gathering facts instead of nurturing dreams of idyllic new townships for industrious and deserving crofters which were, in the Home Secretary's words to Queen Victoria, 'fantastic projects for the restitution of the tribal system and common property in the Highlands ... which have aroused expectations and demands which it will be impossible to satisfy.'

Harcourt was wrong in at least one vital respect. The crofters' 'expectations and demands' had been aroused long before the publication of the Napier Report. When that report resulted in unacceptable and impractical recommendations and consequent governmental inaction, a revival of militant activity was inevitable. Napier's proposals were dead in the water, but the power of the preceding testimony was very much alive.

Once again, the militancy was centred in Skye.

NINE

Skye as an International Symbol of Land Reform

THE HONEYMOON BETWEEN the Napier Commission and the crofters of Skye began to sour after less than a year and ended acrimoniously within 15 months.

If the Highland Land League, or the Highland Land Law Reform Association, was first established at those clandestine meetings in Glendale early in 1882, by 1883 it was up and running among exiles in London. The organisation did not, however, create formal, constitutional branches in the Highlands until 1884.

On 3 January 1884 a news story from London was syndicated throughout the United Kingdom. It reported that 'Mr Michael Davitt and Mr Henry George will in the course of the next few days arrive in London to arrange measures in concert with the land reformers of the metropolis in favour of land nationalisation among the Highland crofters.

'In the course of a few weeks Messrs Davitt and George will proceed together to Skye. Meetings will be held in different areas of disaffection in the Highlands, and it is probable that branches of a Highland Land League will be formed under an organisation scheme similar to that instituted by Mr Davitt when the Irish Land League was started. An enthusiastic response from the Gaelic population is confidently promised by the originators of the movement.'

Michael Davitt of the Irish Land League had become increasingly convinced of two essentials. One was that the answer to the land question was nationalisation. The other was that the answer should be offered not only in Ireland but throughout the rest of the United Kingdom, including of course the Highlands and Islands of Scotland.

Henry George was an American who held broadly similar views. In 1879 George had published in the United States an international bestseller, *Progress and Poverty*, which argued in part that, 'We must make land common property', and whose widespread popular appeal led to his invitation to address interested audiences in Europe.

The fact that both men advertised faraway Skye as a primary venue for the propagation of their views was indicative of the island's reputation by 1884 as a spiritual and intellectual home of British, if not European, land reform. Davitt would eventually reach Skye, but failed to do so in 1884. Henry George did make the journey. In the company of the indefatigable Edward McHugh, who acted as George's lecture agent in Scotland, during the second week of February 1884 'the prophet of San Francisco' spoke to large crowds in Portree, Glendale (where he was chaired by John MacPherson) and Kilmuir (where he was accompanied by John MacPherson).

The gist of Henry George's short speech was the same in each parish. 'A system which gave the whole island of Skye to eleven proprietors, who had all power over its seventeen thousand inhabitants, was wrong, and unjust and downright robbery,' he said. '. . . It was a great fact that, although enormous advances had been made in civilisation, the lot of the toiling masses had not been improved. While landlordism existed it was impossible to relieve poverty.'

In Portree, where he spoke in the evening at the Public School, Henry George was challenged by Lauchlan MacDonald of Skeabost to say what he 'recommended the people to do with the landlords if their lands be taken from them'.

'Mr George replied that he would do with the landlords as the fisherman does with the oyster – open it, take out the fish and throw the shells away.'

There was a sensation in the hall and MacDonald walked out. Henry George had been unaware before offering his analogy that Lauchlan MacDonald had recently removed from his tenants their right to catch shellfish in the shallows around his estate.

In the last week of April 1884 the Glaswegian socialist and land reformer James Shaw-Maxwell also visited Skye, and was also met and accompanied there by John MacPherson. A few days later the secretary of the Highland Land Law Reform Association of London announced that his organisation had formed sub-committees in Ross and Cromarty, Caithness, Edinburgh, Inverness and the islands of Lewis and Skye. All who might be prepared to 'assist the movement' were 'requested to communicate without delay' with their local representative, who in the case of Skye was John MacPherson of Glendale.

Towards the end of June 1884 John MacPherson toured the island of Lewis, addressing crofters throughout that largest of the Hebrides. 'The effect of his oratory,' reported the *Aberdeen People's Journal*, 'seems to have been to unite the crofters in support of the movement for the reform of the land laws. Meanwhile he has returned to Glendale for a short rest during the Communion season, but in September it is expected he will continue his mission by visiting the West Coast . . .'

In August MacPherson was in the Argyllshire island of Mull and in October he returned to Lewis, this time in the company of Alexander MacKenzie and Reverend Donald MacCallum of Waternish. Rent strikes were underway in the Lochs and Uig districts of Lewis and on Thursday, 16 October 1884, 'in the forenoon the crofters kept pouring in [to Stornoway] from all directions, some with pipes, and banners flying. About noon upwards of one thousand were marshalled. They afterwards marched round the town. Many of the banners had striking mottoes . . . The speaking was altogether in Gaelic, and much of it was such as to rouse the people to a great state of excitement. A serious crisis exists in the island.'

In November, both the crisis and John MacPherson returned home to Skye. In October 1884 1,000 crofters on Captain William Fraser's Kilmuir estate, where Norman 'Parnell' Stewart had kindled the first open rebellion in Skye seven years earlier, resolved to go on rent strike. Their argument, they stated, was with factor Alexander MacDonald 'for his many acts of tyranny and his backing of unscrupulous characters [the crofters were referring to Kilmuir's tenant sheep-farmers] who oppressed us in every conceivable way for many years . . .'

Sheriff William Ivory and Chief Constable Alexander McHardy acted promptly. In an attempt to forestall another Braes or Glendale and snuff out early the flame of discontent in Kilmuir, on 30 October they despatched ten policemen under the long-suffering Inspector Malcolm MacDonald to Uig in Kilmuir to maintain the law.

The welcome offered to such expeditions in isolated Skye peninsulas was by 1884 an established tradition. The policemen were met in Uig by hundreds of crofters, who duly drove the officers back to Portree.

To the Inverness-shire authorities, that was the last straw. An entire island, the largest and most celebrated in their domain, was steadily, parish by parish, declaring itself to be at best beyond the law, and at worst in revolution. As the police were unavailable to them in sufficient numbers to restore and maintain order, they once again appealed to the Government for troops. Chief-Constable Alexander McHardy issued a memorandum stating that a 'reign of terror' existed in Skye. Sheriff William Ivory was 'of opinion that the immediate despatch of a gunboat and marines to Skye is absolutely necessary to protect the police and assist them in protecting the property and persons of the lieges in that island'.

This time, William Gladstone's Liberal administration

conceded to the request from Inverness Castle. They did so with manifest reluctance. Lord Advocate John Blair Balfour refused to attempt to prosecute the Kilmuir crofters for deforcing the police at Uig and Staffin because, he opined, the crofters believed the police to be little more than agents for the Highland landowning interest.

Talk of impending invasion swept through Skye and the rest of Britain. On 8 November the *Aberdeen Evening Express* reported that 80 armed police were expected at any time to put ashore in Uig Bay, where they would be met by 1,200 crofters armed with sticks – 'A rumour was current last night that the Glendale crofters are to proceed to the assistance of the Uig men.'

The 80 armed police never arrived in Uig. Instead, 350 professional troops were landed.

In an extraordinary speech to the House of Commons on 14 November 1884, the Home Secretary William Harcourt admitted to despatching soldiers to Skye only under severe political and personal duress.

'With the official responsibility that I have in this matter,' said the Home Secretary, 'hon. Members in the House will feel that I am not free to say all that I think, because I must exercise a certain amount of reserve. But I think I am not acting inconsistently with my duty in this matter in saying . . . [that the crofters of Skye] have long had my deep personal sympathy . . .

'All I can say is, that though there are painful duties connected frequently with the Office which I hold, I have never exercised a duty which I considered incumbent upon me with more personal regret than when I felt myself under the obligation to send a force to support the Local Authority in that part of the country . . .

'I am the first to state and to feel that the employment of the Naval or Military Forces of the Crown in keeping peace in this country, or in any way aiding the civil authority, is in itself an immense evil. It is one to which I am most reluctant to resort, and never would do so unless I was convinced that it was absolutely necessary.

'The preservation of peace, and the exercise of the civil authority, ought to be carried out by the Civil Force, which is the police; and happily in this country, although cases do occasionally occur where the police, not being sufficient, military support has to be given to the police, I take it to be a maxim, subject to very few exceptions, that the Military and Naval Forces ought never, if it can possibly be avoided, to be used for that purpose. And, accordingly, when a few years ago there were disturbances in Skye, and I was pressed by the Local Authorities to send military there, I told them of my reluctance, and declined.'

By November 1884, however, Harcourt considered himself no longer able to decline the requests from Inverness for military support. 'I think there is no doubt,' he continued, 'and the House will take this from me without my going into great detail – that there is a very serious condition of things existing in Skye and the West Highlands generally . . .

'Now, I say alone this hostility towards the police, this determination not to show to them that obedience and that respect for law and order which is common in other parts of England and Scotland, is in itself a very serious symptom. When it comes to this, that in some parts of Skye and the Highlands the police have to be sent to execute the ordinary processes of the law, that is in itself a very serious condition of things.

'At the same time, I say it is very necessary that all classes of the community – and I include in that the Police Committee of the county of Inverness – must understand that the Government cannot undertake to aid the police permanently by military force. And a state of things must be established in which the police shall be able to maintain the public peace, and execute justice within their own territory. The Government make it clearly understood that in giving this support to the police it is as a subsidiary force, and not as a principal force, in the execution of the law. In my opinion, nothing can be greater proof that there is something which requires a remedy than when you are obliged to employ a military force.'

Having established the limits under which the military would be sent to Skye, William Harcourt then launched a fierce attack on what he considered to be the causes of the unrest: the misbehaviour of Sheriff Ivory's 'lieges', the Highland landowners.

'These notices of removal,' said the Home Secretary, 'seem to me to be a source of irritation which is not to be justified at all. That there exists in these districts extreme poverty, in some parts borne for many years with extraordinary patience, I think everybody who is acquainted with those districts must be aware . . .

'Some people say – "Oh, the remedy for this is emigration." Well, Sir, in my opinion, emigration is a very poor remedy indeed. I have myself no sympathy with a policy which improves a country by getting rid of its people. To my mind that is the policy of despair. It is like the old medical treatment of Sangrado, who cured all diseases by blood-letting; but, after all, blood is the life of the body, and the people are the life of the country. I, at all events, do not accept the policy of making a solitude and calling it political economy . . .

'After the sheep farm gave an enormous increase to the rent of the proprietor – an increase without absolutely any expenditure on his part – there was possibly never a better instance of the unearned increment except that which I am going to mention . . .

'Then close upon the sheep-farming came the grouse-shooting rent, which was often, I believe, equal to the sheep-farming rent; therefore, the proprietor found himself in possession of land which rose within a generation from being worth nothing at all to an enormously increased and valuable rental. In more recent years, in my own recollection, there was found a still more valuable thing than the sheep farm and the game rent, and that was the deer forest, over a great part of the county of Ross and a considerable part of the county of Inverness, in the place of both the sheep rent and the game rent.

'Well, what was the result of that? The result was that, while the rent value increased, the grazing of these people [the crofters] disappeared.

'Now, just consider what would have happened if, when these large tracts of land were being turned into sheep farms or into deer forests, yielding, as they did, an enormous increment of rent, there had been a more moderate use of these powers – if, while thousands of acres were taken for these purposes, a few hundreds had everywhere been reserved for the small population of these Highland glens – why, it would not have destroyed the system of sheep-farming at all.

'It would have been perfectly possible to have kept a moderate area which would have been sufficient for this population. They never could have covered the whole of these hills. That, it seems to me, is a thing which might very reasonably and well have been done. We have heard in this debate, and evidence has been given, of townships losing the hills which they had before. Why should townships lose the hills? I have never heard of them having refused to pay rent, except under the influence – I was almost going to say of pardonable excitement.

'But why, if a reasonable rent and a fair rent be offered them, should not these people have the accommodation which might make to them the difference between penury and comparative ease? It is quite unquestionable that it has led in a great degree to the change in the condition of the crofter in the West Highlands. What has become of the crofters' black cattle?

'There is no doubt that they can look back to a time, which they remember themselves, or of which they certainly had a tradition from their fathers, when they had this land, on which they had black cattle, and which, having lost, they have been confined to that little spot in the strath which, when potato disease comes or a bad season, is totally unable to sustain their existence.'

William Harcourt's qualifications for sending military aid to the civil authority, and his radical diagnosis of the roots of the problem – a diagnosis which was almost indistinguishable from that of John Murdoch, Alexander MacKenzie, John MacPherson and the Highland Land League – were understandably obscured by the headline announcement that British troops were being despatched to occupy the British island of Skye.

The press from all over Britain descended on the north-west Highlands. The people of the region waited anxiously to see what form this military incursion would take. The Highland Land League and various ministers urged restraint upon their members and their congregations. On the hills which surrounded Uig Bay, crofters posted sentries with horns to blow the alarm if ships of the Royal Navy appeared on the horizon.

Far away in London a small girl found herself, by happenstance, sharing the excitement at the other end of the operation. Flora MacLeod was five years old in November 1884. She was the granddaughter of Norman, the 25th chief of MacLeod, who had moved from Dunvegan to pursue a civil service career in London following the potato famine in the late 1840s.

Flora's father, Reginald MacLeod, would in time become both a knight and the 27th chief of the clan. He was born in London in 1847. Thirty years later Reginald improved his family's prospects by marrying the daughter of Sir Stafford Northcote, who was at the time Chancellor of the Exchequer and would later become Foreign Secretary. A result of that marriage was that Flora MacLeod, who would also become the 28th and first female chief of Clan MacLeod between 1935 and 1976, was born at Number 10 Downing Street, which Stafford Northcote's large family borrowed from his single, widowed Prime Minister.

In 1884, however, Stafford Northcote's Conservative Party was out of office and the MacLeods were living in Hobart Place in Belgravia. Dame Flora, as she became, would always insist that her earliest memory was of shortly after dawn in Hobart Place on a November day in 1884, when she saw from her nursery window 'an officer on horseback, wearing full-dress uniform, canter to the door of her house. He had come to tell her father that Sir Garnet Wolseley wished to see him at the Foreign Office. The Government was sending troops to quell the Glendale uprising in Skye, and wanted Reginald MacLeod's advice on the best place to land. The rush of hasty footsteps on the stairs, and the brilliant figure on horseback galloping away . . .'

Unless the incident happened earlier and Reginald MacLeod was summoned to assist with contingency planning, whoever MacLeod advised at the Foreign Office about the logistics of invading Skye, it was not General Sir Garnet Wolseley. Wolseley was the Adjutant-General to the Forces, but in November 1884 he was on his way to Khartoum in a doomed attempt to relieve General Charles George Gordon's besieged Sudanese garrison. There is nonetheless little reason to doubt the gist of Flora MacLeod's recollection, which was that the Government called upon a MacLeod of Dunvegan who was conveniently living in London for advice about the conditions in Skye.

Whether or not it was thanks to the wisdom of Reginald MacLeod, the 1884 occupation began with both naval and merchant vessels entering Portree Bay on Saturday, 15 and Sunday, 16 November.

That Saturday John MacPherson, with 50 other Glendale men, travelled to Uig to urge their fellow crofters in Kilmuir not to mount an armed resistance. Speaking in Gaelic, MacPherson persuaded the Kilmuir militants 'to confine their agitation within constitutional limits . . . amidst the gloom there were some rays of hope, and by legal agitation he believed they would be able to convince the authorities that they had tangible grievances that must be put right . . . It was not the shedding of blood that could procure them any of the objects they had in view.'

After a two-hour meeting John MacPherson then hurried in the evening from Uig to Portree, where Sheriff Ivory, Sheriff-Substitute Speirs, Chief Constable McHardy and other dignitaries were waiting in the company of 40 Inverness-shire policemen aboard the steamer *Lochiel*. MacPherson assured Ivory that the Uig crofters were prepared to meet and discuss matters with the authorities, and that any crofters charged with any offence would 'give themselves up to justice at Portree'. '[It] is owing to MacPherson's counsels,' reported the *Glasgow Herald*, 'that the crofters have changed their attitude of violent hostility to one of humble submission.' Sheriff Ivory expressed his satisfaction and went ashore to telegram William Harcourt. John MacPherson then retired to the Portree Hotel, where he sat for sketches by an artist from the *Illustrated London News*.

On the same Saturday night John MacPherson wrote and despatched a letter back 'To the Crofters of Kilmuir'. Their resolution to accede to the law had, he said, 'afforded [William Ivory] much pleasure . . . The Sheriff further declared himself satisfied, and said it would be unnecessary for your deputation to come the long distance from Uig to Portree . . . we cannot say that the expeditionary force is not to visit Uig as well as the other parts of the island as was originally intended.'

The small gunboat *Forester* and the MV *Lochiel* were joined in Portree Bay by the main force shortly before noon on the following day, Sunday, 16 November. The troopship HMS *Assistance* arrived with 350 red-coated marines and 100 blue-jackets, or battle-ready naval seamen. No matter how conciliatory was the message delivered by John MacPherson, as he had told his colleagues in Kilmuir, the military expedition was under way and would not be withdrawn.

It was a show of force rather than a punitive expedition. The occupation would last for seven months, during which time not a shot was fired at a human being in Skye, although the local game was not so lucky – the captain of the *Assistance* immediately set the tone by going ashore for a few hours' shooting on the moor around Portree. The response of the people of Skye nonetheless veered between outrage and fear. A Kilmuir shoemaker, John

MacLeod, said that 'he never thought he should have lived to see the day when an armed force would be sent to their beloved island, as there did not exist throughout the whole British empire a people more attached to their beloved Queen . . . The Queen's sacred person was as safe among Highlanders as when she leant on the breast of her mother. The Highlanders of Skye had been grossly misrepresented; they had been charged with crimes that had no existence whatsoever.'

On the morning of Monday, 17 November, as MacPherson had warned the Kilmuir men, the *Assistance*, the *Forester* and the *Lochiel* sailed around the north of Skye from Portree to Uig. 'There was no demonstration whatsoever,' reported the *Glasgow Herald*, 'on any part of the coast.' The village of Uig itself 'was found in a state of the most perfect peace, with every crofter minding his own business'.

Unlike generals Wolseley and Gordon in Sudan, the commanders of the military expedition to Skye could find no enemies to fight. This evidently perplexed them. The afternoon drew on with the ships motionless in invasion formation in Uig Bay – the *Forester* between the shore and the *Assistance*, covering with her guns any attempted landings from the troop-ship. Sheriff Ivory broke the deadlock by recommending that seven policemen be sent from the *Lochiel* to spend the night in Uig, where they should be guarded by 70 marines. As night fell small boats took those men ashore and, under the curious gaze of a few women and boys, the policemen and redcoats marched to their temporary lodgings in the school. 'Not a word of disapproval or otherwise was uttered by the few onlookers who here and there lined the road as the smart little procession of armed men treaded its way . . .'

On the following day the marines and policemen marched, in full battle order with bugles blowing, over the high pass to Staffin on the east coast of the estate, where their presence was met with the same stunning indifference. '[Every] crofter met,' wrote the man from the *Glasgow Herald*, 'ridiculed the idea' of

250 marines being sent to the scattered population of Staffin. 'One man, it was said, would have answered the purpose of the 250, for in him the crofters say they would have respected all the same the authority of Her Majesty's Government, which they reiterate almost to weariness they have no desire to resist ... That they still decline to look upon the constabulary as anything else than the emissaries of a body of landlords sitting in Inverness they make no secret.' Fifty marines were deposited in Staffin Lodge and advised by their officers not to annoy the natives.

The military expedition then moved on to Dunvegan, and Glendale.

The *Forester* had been joined by another gunboat, the *Banterer*. On Friday, 28 November, those two vessels put ashore at Colbost jetty the detachment of those remaining marines who had not been left guarding policemen in lodges and schools elsewhere in northern Skye. The troops, and the constables under their protection, then marched in the footsteps of Donald MacTavish, James MacRaild and Inspector Malcolm MacDonald around the shore of Loch Dunvegan and up Cnoc an t-Sìthein towards the broad valley of Glendale.

Halfway up Cnoc an t-Sìthein a wide, shallow natural amphitheatre has been carved by prehistoric ice from the side of the glen. In that amphitheatre the redcoats could see a gathering of hundreds of Glendale crofters – the *Aberdeen People's Journal* reported that 'by two o'clock at least 600 persons had assembled'. Sheriff Ivory held tight to his copy of the Riot Act. Two companies of marines and one of marine artillery positioned themselves facing the crofters. Local lore had it that redcoats were placed on the low tops of the surrounding hills. Rifles at the ready, the soldiers walked nervously up Cnoc an t-Sìthein towards the assembly. As they drew closer the crofters issued a loud cheer.

At first the soldiers understood that cheer to be at best a shout of derision, and at worst a battle-cry. Luckily their senior officers, one of whom was riding a donkey and smoking a cigar, remained cool, because it was neither.

John MacPherson and the Glendale men – who had met on the previous evening to discuss their response to the imminent incursion – were conducting an open air meeting of their land league. The meeting had begun with an elderly local blind man reciting a prayer. As the troops came into view MacPherson urged his people 'to be courageous and not afraid, because they had never broken the law. He assured his hearers that meetings would continue to be held, and agitation persisted in, no matter how many policemen and marines the Government might send.'

That statement of defiance provoked the cheer. The gathering of crofters paid no attention whatsoever to the 100 redcoats and policemen who crept past them up Cnoc an t-Sìthein. Occasional jeers from the troops went unacknowledged and unanswered. The military expedition continued unmolested to Hamara Lodge, where it deposited twenty-five marines and six policemen before the remainder returned to Colbost pier, and then to HMS *Assistance*.

The tactics were plain. Small numbers of police officers under the protection of much larger numbers of soldiers would be billeted at the heart of trouble spots throughout northern Skye, leaving a core force of marines anchored in Portree Bay, ready to reinforce their comrades as required. The police officers would then be able to keep the peace, reassert their dignity and whenever necessary escort sheriff officers and messengers-at-arms in their serving of writs.

There were no major disturbances during the presence of the marines in Skye. Home Secretary William Harcourt had made it clear that the military would not be in Skye to enforce the law – that was the job of the police – and that the soldiers would be in the island only for a limited period of time, to oversee the re-establishment of order and allow Sheriff Ivory, Chief Constable McHardy and the Inverness-shire constabulary to catch their collective breath.

There was no open conflict during the military occupation because the crofters and, more crucially, the crofters' leaders such as John MacPherson, had neither the desire nor the lack of sense to engage with armed marines who they knew, in any case, would soon be gone. For a few months the cottage economies of Glendale and Kilmuir estates experienced a small boom as the people sold eggs, fish and meat to the soldiers in their midst. Fishing girls flirted with redcoats; ragged boys followed them around the place; the marines found themselves among the most courteous and hospitable people in Britain and wondered why on earth they were there.

The local authorities nonetheless succeeded in serving several summonses, despite the fact that there were no serious outstanding summons to serve, and despite the fact that both Harcourt and Balfour had warned the landowners against this form of action, had condemned eviction orders, and had ordered the Highland upper classes to use this period of stabilisation to put their own estates in order before legislation was passed through Parliament in the wake of the Napier Report.

But the rent strikes continued and Sheriff Ivory persisted in arresting as many offenders as possible. In late December 1884 he brought nine men from Kilmuir to trial in Portree, where he was singled out by a large crowd for sustained abuse. At the same time Ivory sent a messenger-at-arms into Glendale. There, despite the presence of the marines and policemen at Hamara Lodge, who failed to become involved, the messenger-at-arms was driven back to Colbost by hundreds of people before he could issue a single warrant.

Sheriff William Ivory then made plans to impose himself on Glendale.

Well before first light, at 6 a.m. on Thursday, 29 January 1885, the *Assistance* and the *Lochiel* once again put into Loch Dunvegan. Twenty-five policemen and two hundred marines were landed at Colbost jetty and marched in darkness over to Glendale. There, as dawn broke, they arrested six crofters at their homes. A crowd of 200 to 300 people quickly gathered and hurled abuse at the police. John MacPherson appeared on the scene, 'immediately sought out Sheriff Ivory, and protested in the strongest manner against such a force being brought to the glen to arrest parties whom he declared to be guiltless of any crime, laying the whole blame on the police, who he alleged had made lying statements regarding the breaking down of fences and other outrages'.

To the amusement of the couple of journalists present, MacPherson and Ivory then engaged in a heated debate of the land question, 'the Sheriff maintaining that the present demands of the crofters were unreasonable, and "The Martyr" contending that the rights of the people to the land exceeded those of the proprietors'. John MacPherson had just returned from a lecture tour and Ivory suggested that all of this agitation was a profitable exercise for the man from Lower Milovaig.

'Wouldn't you just like to get hold of me?' said John MacPherson.

'Wouldn't I just,' replied Sheriff William Ivory.

John MacPherson said, with the marines and journalists listening attentively, that it was a good thing that Sheriff Ivory had no power to shoot the crofters.

'I replied,' William Ivory would later report, 'that he was quite mistaken: that I had the power; that if I considered it to be my duty to give the order to fire, it would be obeyed.'

MacPherson then turned his attention to the colonel in charge of the two hundred marines, and following a civilised conversation with the officer the six crofters were led away by the police and their military escort to Colbost, the MV *Lochiel*, and the jail in Portree. Ivory's party proceeded on the following day to Valtos on the Kilmuir estate, but the Staffin men had been forewarned and six of the eight suspects took to the hills 'and remained concealed all day'.

To the disgust of the people of Skye, Ivory continued throughout February to cut a swathe through Glendale and

Kilmuir. Increasing numbers of people gathered at Portree quayside as each fresh small batch of prisoners was landed. They 'vigorously hissed the Sheriff and the policemen, and heartily cheered the crofters and marines ... During the day Sheriff Ivory and the policemen were hissed in the streets [of Portree], and the feeling against the constables appeared to be increasingly bitter.'

In fact almost all of those arrested by William Ivory – including the indefatigable Norman 'Parnell' Stewart of Valtos – were sooner or later dismissed from the Portree court for lack of evidence against them, and sent home without trial by Sheriff-Substitute Peter Speirs, who consequently won a great deal of respect from the crofters of Skye as 'a man of clear judgement'. It is likely that Sheriff Ivory's conversation with John MacPherson in Glendale on the morning of 29 January had proved to be a turning point.

The sheriff of Inverness-shire, along with all other officers of the law, was supposed to be apolitical. For a number of years William Ivory's actions had suggested that he was very far from politically neutral, and that he considered it to be an essential part of his job to uphold the interests of the Highland landowning class.

It was one thing for the sheriff's actions at Braes and elsewhere to suggest such a bias. It was quite another for him openly to admit it in front of journalists, policemen and military officers, as Ivory had done while debating the land question with John MacPherson in Glendale. It was also unwise of the sheriff to state that he would like very much to arrest John MacPherson, and that he had the power to order crofters to be shot. Lord Advocate John Balfour was asked embarrassing questions in the House of Commons about the conduct of Sheriff William Ivory.

They were questions which Balfour was unable to answer, leaving Donald Macfarlane MP to conclude that, 'Whether the Highlands were disturbed or not, the administration of the law should, as far as possible, be above suspicion. That was not the case . . . All that they asked for was a strict investigation; and if on that it was proved that a high officer of the law had misused his position to terrorize the people – as he had good reason to believe he had – then he hoped Her Majesty's Government would make an example of him that would be remembered by the Highlands and by all Scotland . . . The people did not believe in him or his justice; and it did not matter whether he was just and impartial or not. So long as the people did not believe in his justice and impartiality he was unfit to be an officer of the Crown.'

Sheriff Ivory would never be restrained, let alone relieved of his office. But following the acquittals of his crofter prisoners at Portree Sheriff Court and the exchanges in the House of Commons the military expedition to Skye was slowly wound down. On 20 April 1885 all but 70 of the marines sailed away from Portree on HMS *Assistance*. According to the *Dundee Advertiser*, 'The Marines were heartily cheered as they left the quay, and replied by calling for cheers for the crofters.' Two months later the remaining marines and all of the extra policemen were brought from the outlying districts back to Portree. On 24 June 1885 they left Skye for Inverness, from whose railway station the marines made their way back to Portsmouth and the policemen 'returned to their own respective stations'. There was, headlined the *Dundee Evening Telegraph*, 'Tranquillity in Skye'.

TEN

The End of the Clearances and the Dawn of Community Ownership

THERE WAS NOT, in the continuing absence of legislation following the Napier Report, tranquillity in Skye. Neither was there much tranquillity in the rest of the United Kingdom.

In June 1885, as the troops were leaving Skye, William Gladstone resigned as Prime Minister and conceded Number 10 Downing Street to the Conservative Robert Gascoyne-Cecil, 3rd Marquess of Salisbury. Lord Salisbury governed with a minority administration until a general election was held in November and December 1885.

It was a momentous general election in the north of Scotland. Gladstone's voting Reform Act of 1884 had, as we have seen, increased the electorate by about 6,000,000 men. Among those 6,000,000 men were almost all of the crofters of the Highlands and Islands who had previously been unfranchised. The number of voters in Argyllshire rose suddenly from 3,299 men to 10,011 men. The numbers in Ross-shire, which included the large Hebridean island of Lewis, rose from 1,664 to 10,265. The numbers in Inverness-shire, which included the islands of Harris, Skye and Uist, rose from 1,851 to 9,330.

The land leaguers saw and took their chance. Five 'Crofters' Candidates' were presented to the electorates of Sutherlandshire, Ross-shire, Caithness-shire, Argyllshire and Inverness-shire.

They were successful everywhere but in Sutherland. Donald Macfarlane, the land reformer and former Irish Nationalist member for Carlow, became the crofters' MP for Argyllshire, and Charles Fraser Mackintosh, the land reformer, member of the Napier Commission and former member for Inverness Burghs, became the crofters' MP for rural Inverness-shire.

It was a remarkable display of solidarity and intent by the Highland crofting community. Their representatives were suddenly single-issue parliamentarians. Their function in the House of Commons would be to press for suitable legislation in the spirit of the Napier Report. That may be why, as William Gladstone moved once again into Number 10 Downing Street, and William Harcourt returned to the Home Office in January 1886, a crofters' act moved to the very top of their agenda. They were not to know, early in 1886, that the crofters' act would be the only significant legislation passed by Gladstone's third administration.

Following the military occupation of Skye and then the premiership of the Tory Lord Salisbury, Highland landowners had allowed themselves to relax their guard. Suddenly, as 1886 dawned, they heard once again the beating of the wings of land reform. They and their agents mobilised. They might have guessed that they were dealing with a prime minister and a home secretary who were by then thoroughly fed up with Highland lairds.

Between December 1884 and January 1885, while the troops were beginning their residence in Skye, there had been an exchange of letters between Donald Cameron of Lochiel, the Lord Advocate John Balfour, the Home Secretary William Harcourt and the Prime Minister William Gladstone.

Cameron, speaking on behalf of his fellow 'proprietors who have crofting tenants', told Harcourt that the landowners were prepared to consider such reforms as an arbitrated rent, leases of 10 to 30 years, the payment of compensation for crofters' improvements to their rented properties and the leasing of some

'additional land' to the grazings of crofters who could afford to
rent it. The Highland proprietors would concede those points
in exchange for no further threats of an 'Irish Land Act' which
would take 'all power out of the hands of the landlord'. The
crofters' 'ardent longing for more land', said Cameron, must in
the absence of a nationalising administration or a sympathetic,
altruistic body of landowners 'not only remain unsatisfied, but
rendered absolutely hopeless'.

The landowners were also keen to point out that while it
might be possible to administer Ireland as a discrete political
entity, the same did not apply to the adjacent shires of Scotland,
England and Wales. If certain fresh rights and benefits were to
be given to tenant smallholders in the Highlands and Islands
who happened to be called crofters, should they not also be
extended to tenants in Fifeshire, Galloway, Yorkshire and
Surrey?

That pragmatic consideration struck a chord in the legal brain
of the Lord Advocate. 'If the necessities of the persons residing in
a particular locality,' responded John Blair Balfour, 'were held to
raise an objection, enforceable by Parliament, upon the proprietors of land in the vicinity, to let to such persons so much land
as they needed for their comfortable maintenance, this would
imply an acceptance of the doctrine that the land of the country
should, as regards occupancy, be periodically redistributed . . .
And if such a principle was sanctioned in the Highlands and
Islands of Scotland, it is difficult to see how Parliament could
refuse to extend it to the Lowlands and to England.'

Balfour nonetheless considered that Cameron and his friends
were offering too little at that advanced state in proceedings, when the Government had been obliged to send troops
to protect them from their tenants. 'I believe,' said the Lord
Advocate, 'that if, a few years ago, the proprietors of Highland
estates had universally, or even very generally, offered to their
crofters such terms as Lochiel proposes, legislation would have
been unnecessary; but I greatly fear that for this purpose the

offer now comes too late. It appears to me that the Government and the Parliament are practically committed to some legislation on the Crofter question, and that such legislation is expected by the country . . .

'Then it is to be kept in view,' continued Balfour, 'that even if the existing Highland proprietors universally agreed to the proposed scheme they could not bind their successors to follow it out, and the insecurity, which is one of the evils of the crofter's position, though mitigated, would not be removed.'

The existing Highland proprietors did in fact almost universally agree to Cameron of Lochiel's proposed scheme. At a massed rally of the landowning gentry in Inverness on 14 January 1885 some 50 proprietors and their appointed agents met to discuss ways of deterring and pre-empting serious land reform by the Liberal Government. Lochiel of course was there, as was his fellow Napier Commissioner Sir Kenneth MacKenzie of Gairloch. There was Captain, by then Major, Fraser of Kilmuir. Flora MacLeod's father, and the heir to his clan chieftainship, Reginald MacLeod was up from London. The Glendale factor John Robertson attended, in the company of representatives of the big estates in the Western Isles.

The meeting carefully endorsed each of Lochiel's suggestions. Where 'suitable opportunities offer' they would, they said, voluntarily increase the size of the holdings of crofters who could afford both the extra stock and the increased rental. Crofters who were not in rent arrears (or, obviously, on rent strike, which disqualified most of north Skye) might be offered leases of between 19 and 30 years. And if a crofter relinquished his holding he would be compensated for 'permanent improvements', such as the building of a house or byre.

But it was too late in January 1885, and it would also be too late in the following year. Balfour and Harcourt agreed that there had to be legislation, not only to satisfy the public mood but also to bind the landowners to their assurances.

There was to be a Crofters' Act. The only remaining questions

concerned its shape and its radicalism. As surely as the disturbances in Glendale in 1883 had led to the Napier Commission,
the sending of troops to Kilmuir and Glendale in 1884 ensured
the creation of crofting legislation.

William Gladstone himself weighed into the discussion by
recommending that the new legislation should include 'a fixity
or stability of tenure . . . for all lettings within the Act'. The
Prime Minister also thought that the difficulties encountered
by penurious crofters in stocking extra land were exaggerated
and that crofters were perfectly capable of organising their
own assets. '[I]f those who are to enjoy the grazings were a
promiscuous body,' wrote Gladstone to Harcourt, 'it would
be dangerous and harsh to introduce anything like the rule of
common responsibility. But they are a people united by tradition, by neighbourhood, often by blood, by agitation, as it might
now be added, and always by common interest . . .'

Gladstone also happily answered the doubts of Cameron
of Lochiel, Harcourt and Balfour about the 'serious difficulty'
of a Land Bill 'extending beyond the Highland parishes to all
Scotland, and if to all Scotland, then . . . to England also', and
thereby setting a precedent which would endanger the wider
national landholding interests.

'Now, in my view,' said Gladstone, 'a Land Bill for the crofter
parishes is just as well as politic; but I doubt whether it is just
that the need of such a Bill in such parishes should be made, or
allowed to become, the cause of altering the land system for the
rest of the country; where the matter ought to be judged on its
own merits, and not to be prejudged by the adoption of certain
provisions to meet a case not only actually, but historically,
exceptional . . . [T]he crofter's title to demand the interference
of Parliament,' argued the Prime Minister, ' . . . is not because
they are poor, or because there are too many of them, or because
they want more land to support their families, but because those
whom they represent had rights of which they have been surreptitiously deprived to the injury of the community.'

William Gladstone was too learned a politician not to be aware that agricultural communities in the rest of Scotland and England had also been 'surreptitiously deprived' of their common land during the previous two centuries. But if he was too late to stop the Enclosures, he could at least preserve the remaining small-holders of northern and western Scotland from a similar fate.

Within his cabinet there were of course differences. The Marquess of Hartington, a former leader of the Liberal Party who would shortly inherit the Duchy of Devonshire and who served as Secretary of State for War until 1885, was as opposed to Gladstone's extension of land rights to Highland crofters as he was to the Prime Minister's attempts to accommodate Irish nationalism, and for similar reasons. As well as his obvious identification with the landowning fraternity, Hartington considered that any legislation in favour of the crofters was simply demonstrating 'sympathy with law-breaking'.

On the other hand, the President of the Board of Trade Joseph Chamberlain was at that time an ardent supporter of improved rights for agricultural workers throughout Britain. Chamberlain would visit the Highlands and Islands in later months and years to express his sympathy with the crofters' cause. In the meantime he urged William Harcourt to ignore the overtures of the Marquess of Hartington and push a radical Crofters' Bill through the House of Commons.

According to Lewis Harcourt, the Home Secretary's son, when William Harcourt persuaded the cabinet to accept his draft Crofters' Bill in March 1885, having been 'opposed by Hartington as going too far, and by Chamberlain for not going far enough', Harcourt 'suggested that they had better split the difference'. That was probably too glib a version of events, but it contained a modicum of truth. When Hartington observed his cabinet colleagues' collective and unanimous approval of the Bill, again according to Lewis Harcourt, the Marquess 'only asked, "Is it very bad?" meaning very Radical – the words are synonymous in his vocabulary'.

That was the Crofters' Bill, which was abandoned during the parliamentary upheavals of the summer of 1885 but was adopted once again by Gladstone and Harcourt early in 1886. It was not 'very Radical' but it was in some ways radical enough. Harcourt avoided the possibility of the crofters' contagion spreading throughout the rest of the United Kingdom by limiting the Bill to the counties in which the Napier Commission had taken evidence. The Crofters' Bill would therefore apply in Argyllshire and its islands, Caithness, Cromarty, Inverness-shire (which included Skye, Harris, Uist, Barra and several smaller Hebrides), Ross-shire (which included the island of Lewis), Sutherlandshire and the northern islands of Orkney and Shetland. Landowners in the more fertile east and south of Scotland, as well as in England, could sleep easily in their beds.

The Bill offered security of tenure to all crofters, no matter how large or small their crofts, at a rental to be adjudicated by an independent Crofters' Commission. Crofts could not be bought and sold but crofters were permitted to bequeath their tenancies to a person of their choice. The Bill also compelled landlords to compensate departing crofters or their families 'for any permanent improvements'. At a stroke, those clauses answered the crofters' more modest demands for the 'Three Fs', and put an end to arbitrary evictions and to the Highland Clearances. It was purely, in William Harcourt's words, 'An Act to amend the Law relating to the Tenure of Land by Crofters in the Highlands and Islands of Scotland, and for other purposes relating thereto.'

What the Bill did not offer, to the satisfaction of Cameron of Lochiel and the Marquess of Hartington but the frustration of the land leagues and the newly-elected Crofters' MPs, was the wholesale redistribution of such land as Waterstein on the Glendale estate. Any addition to crofters' holdings should be by the consent of their landowner. The Crofters' Commission could intervene only when proprietors 'have refused to let such crofters available land on reasonable terms for enlarging the holdings of such crofters', and even then they were not permitted to reapportion land which was deemed to be in use, such as a sheep farm or even 'a deer forest, or . . . a grouse moor or other sporting purpose'. That clause not only ensured that most land-hungry crofters would remain unsatisfied; it also failed to address the most basic needs of thousands of landless cottars.

So when the Houses of Commons and Lords passed the Crofters' Holdings (Scotland) Act in June 1886, the Crofters' MPs voted against it and land reformers in the Highlands and elsewhere considered that the war was far from won. Their cry of 'the land for the people' had been ignored. On 23 June 1886 the Kilmuir Land League passed resolutions 'expressing dissatisfaction with the Crofters' Bill as utterly inadequate to meet the requirements and the demands of the crofters . . .'

In September the fourth annual conference of the Highland Land Law Reform Association, which was held at Bonar Bridge in Sutherlandshire, heard that 'the Crofters Act was no settlement of the question', and was told by John MacPherson that 'The Celtic race had the first claims on the British Government and the first right to the possession of the country, for they were its aboriginal inhabitants. Their right was Divine, and they meant to stick to it, for they wished to live on the lands of their native country.'

By that time William Gladstone's Liberal Government had fallen once again and a general election in July 1886 had been won by the Marquess of Salisbury's Conservative Party. This time, Salisbury would hold office for a further six years. They were years during which no further Highland land reform was possible. Instead, William Ivory's view of Highland affairs found more receptive ears in Government, and the sheriff of Inverness-shire exploited his good fortune.

Although most Liberal ministers had come to regard the military occupation of Skye in 1884 and 1885 as a waste of time and money, Sheriff Ivory did not. To him the expedition had been a welcome endorsement of his authority. Although his attempted prosecutions had come to nothing, the presence of hundreds of marines had at least allowed Ivory and the constabulary to travel throughout Skye without harassment. At best – and there is no doubt that Ivory thought in such terms – it had evoked an overdue fear and loathing in the crofting communities. Chief Constable Alexander McHardy was less convinced and more concerned by the apparent politicisation of his force. The two men would fall out over that and other matters, but Ivory always held the upper hand.

William Ivory was also aware that the passing of the Crofters' Act offered an opportunity to divide the community between ordinary working families who were happy enough to be given security of tenure, and militant agitators who wanted the earth. Before June 1886 the agitators had held the high ground, as was evidenced most dramatically by the landslide victories of crofters' candidates in the general election at the end of 1885. But in the general election of July 1886, a month after the Crofters' Act became law, Donald Macfarlane was defeated in Argyllshire. Roderick Macdonald lost interest in the struggle and, while still representing Ross-shire, became a coroner in Middlesex. Gavin Clark of Caithness rejoined the Liberal Party and was re-elected as their candidate. Charles Fraser Mackintosh was returned unopposed in Inverness-shire, but then surveyed the ruins of the Crofters' Party and joined the Liberal Unionist Party. There would never again be a 'Crofters' MP' elected in the Highlands and Islands. The Liberals, who had passed the Crofters' Act which was condemned by the Crofters' MPs, were instead the main political beneficiaries of their Act of 1886.

The implication was that the Crofters' Act had succeeded where 350 marines had failed. It had pacified large areas of the Highlands and Islands, including Skye. It had delivered the Three Fs which such militants as Edward McHugh had discovered years earlier to be the modest aspiration of most Highland crofters. The Glendale man who had called for 'Fixity of tenure; Enlarged holdings; Fair rent fixed by law courts; Compensation;

and Power to buy holdings' was satisfied on three of his five counts and, after years of disruption, was prepared to wait for the other two.

That Glendale man was not of course completely content, and several of his neighbours were still anxious to pursue the land struggle. Sheriff William Ivory rolled up his sleeves and prepared once again to engage with the 'agitators'.

One of the sheriff's first priorities was to break the rent strikes which still continued in Glendale, Kilmuir and elsewhere. The non-payment of rent had become an established part of crofting life in northern Skye. It was a congenial way of simultaneously expressing protest and saving money. It was an article of faith among many crofters. When in the autumn of 1886 false rumours were spread that John MacPherson had resumed paying his rent, the 'Martyr' had vehemently to deny any such apostasy. Rent strikes had, for a variety of reasons, never been properly punished by the law. The security of tenure established by the Crofters' Act might have specifically exempted those who defaulted on their rent, but the spirit of the Act was plain: it would take a particularly foolhardy landowner or factor to attempt to evict a crofting family for any reason after June 1886.

That was not good enough for Sheriff Ivory's landowning employers, and it was unacceptable to Ivory himself. In September 1886 Ivory met with the Conservative Secretary of State for Scotland, Arthur Balfour, whose father and grandfather had owned and cleared of its people the family's shooting estate at Strathconon in Ross-shire. Arthur Balfour (who was not a close relative of Gladstone's Lord Advocate John Blair Balfour) agreed to send a gunboat and marines to Skye to assist with the collection of overdue rents and rates.

This second invasion of Skye by 75 marines and a variety of different vessels in the autumn and winter of 1886 arrived in Portree Bay, where Sheriff Ivory was greeted with the usual chorus of boos and catcalls from assembled inhabitants. The enforcement almost immediately resulted in the 'poinding', or confiscation, of the peatstacks and hayricks – articles which were essential for survival – of Glendale crofters who were summoned to Portree court to answer for rent arrears, before they had been found guilty of a single offence. No Skye carter was willing to carry away the stacks – it was after all early winter, and removing a crofter's source of fuel and animal fodder would have been a form of death sentence – so Ivory hired an east coast carrier. Luckily, few of the peats and little of the hay was carried off before the Glendale crofters were dismissed from Portree court.

In a similar vengeful vein, the expedition also satisfied William Ivory's self-confessed longstanding desire to 'get hold' of John MacPherson.

Ivory had undoubtedly nursed a grievance about the fact that MacPherson had been able to dictate the terms of his own arrest in Glendale early in 1883. In November 1886, the Glendale Martyr was given no such opportunity.

At midnight on Friday, 12 November 1886, one of the most bizarre series of events in the entire Crofters' War got underway. A detachment of police and troops was quietly landed in Glendale from HMS *Jackal* and HMS *Seahorse* in Loch Pooltiel. Under the direction of Sheriff William Ivory the men picked their way through the gloom to the home of John MacPherson in Lower Milovaig. 'On their arrival there,' reported the *Aberdeen Journal*, 'the "martyr" was in bed, but he was soon aroused and immediately taken in charge.

'Macpherson offered no objection to going with the police, and in a short time was in readiness to accompany the officers. He was at once brought aboard the gunboat. The arrest of MacPherson was effected at that early hour without the knowledge of any of the inhabitants, and consequently no excitement was caused.'

Sheriff Ivory, his troops, his policemen and his celebrated prisoner then sailed northwards and around the coast of Skye to Staffin on the Kilmuir estate. There, in the afternoon, a squadron of policemen was put ashore and walked to the house of the

Valtos schoolteacher, where they arrested the schoolteacher's houseguest, Reverend Donald MacCallum, the Waternish Church of Scotland minister who was temporarily standing in for his absent Staffin colleague at Stenscholl Parish Church.

MacCallum, a native of Argyllshire who had been called to a congregation in Skye in 1884, was a well-known 37–year-old land reformer and associate of John MacPherson. He attended land league meetings and mass gatherings. At one famous open-air assembly by the Fairy Bridge at the foot of the Waternish peninsula in 1884, Reverend Donald MacCallum had told hundreds of crofters, 'The land is our birth-right, even as the air, the light of the sun, and water belong to us as our birth-right.

'Man cannot live without a part of the land. We cannot go up with the birds and take up our abode beyond the clouds. We cannot go down to the bottom of the sea and live with the whales. And even could we, the lairds would claim us as their property, as they claim the birds and the fishes. They are the lords of sky, earth and sea. Often was I thinking of the wilderness of the people who inhabit foreign lands, into which a white man never entered. Often did I think that an armed force should be sent to open up these lands for us. I often lamented that we could not even see our God's wonderful work in those regions.

'But I did not consider that our own lands were being closed up, and that soon we could not see our God's wonderful work in our own lands. I did not consider that soon it would be necessary to send an armed force to open up our own land. If the law can keep us from any part of the land, it can keep us from the whole. If the law that can do that is right, then God created us in vain with bodies that cannot live without a part of the earth. Do you know why there are no sun-light leaguers? It is because the sun cannot be bought and sold.'

Reverend Donald MacCallum was therefore a nuisance both to the civil and ecclesiastical authorities. The latter devoted a good deal of time to persuading him to devote himself solely to the teaching of the Gospel, without much success. On the afternoon of Saturday, 13 November 1886, the former arrested him.

While Donald MacCallum was being taken into custody at Valtos, the vessel containing Sheriff Ivory and John MacPherson made its way to Portree, where they arrived at about 6.30 p.m. Word of the events of the previous 19 hours had by then spread around the island and the usual large crowd was assembled at Portree quayside. 'How are you, John?,' cried a voice from the crowd. 'Cheer up old man.'

'John MacPherson is all right,' came the confident reply from the martyr, 'no fear of him.'

The crowd followed the police and their prisoner to the police office, where 'three cheers for John MacPherson' were heartily given. A messenger despatched from Glendale to arrange bail found no shortage of volunteers in Portree, but they were all informed that bail was impossible as MacPherson had not been judicially examined, had not been committed for trial and was consequently ineligible for bail.

Some hours later, when all was quiet at midnight on that Saturday, a carriage pulled up at the County Buildings in Portree and disgorged several policemen and Reverend Donald MacCallum, who was promptly taken to join John MacPherson in the cells. When the news of that second arrest swept Portree in the following Sunday morning, 'much indignation [was] expressed at Mr MacCallum's being detained in the cells when he could have been in custody in a private house or hotel until his judicial examination took place'.

The charges against both MacPherson and MacCallum were specious and unsustainable, as Sheriff Ivory must have known. In the previous month, October 1886, Donald MacCallum had chaired a local land league meeting at Colbost – ironically, one of the meetings at which John MacPherson had been obliged to deny breaking the rent strike. As a result of statements allegedly made at that meeting, John MacPherson and Reverend Donald MacCallum were arrested on suspicion of incitement to violence and incitement to breaking the law. Even if the charges had any foundation – and it was yet to be established that going on rent strike was a criminal offence – witnesses for the prosecution from that Colbost meeting would be impossible to find.

Reverend MacCallum was released without charge on the following Monday morning. Sheriff Ivory managed to keep John MacPherson in the Portree cells for a full seven days, until the next weekend, when he also was released without charge.

After the marines had once again withdrawn, the issue of unpaid rent was settled by an unprecedented agency. As a matter of urgency the Crofters' Commission which had been established by the Crofters' Act conducted a review of croft rents throughout Skye. The commissioners determined that every single crofter in the island had been at best overcharged and at worst rack-rented by his landowner. In some districts, such as Kilmuir and Glendale, the Crofters' Commission reduced rents by up to a third and cancelled two-thirds of all supposed arrears.

That was not only regarded by the crofters of Skye as a form of justification of their rent strikes, and of the insurrections which had followed. It was also the first practical demonstration of the Crofters' Act of 1886 making a positive impact on their lives. The payment of reduced rents was resumed. All of the Skyemen arrested by Sheriff Ivory were, like Donald MacCallum and John MacPherson, either released without charge or let off with admonitory sentences. Land hunger would not go away. In many parts of the Highlands the land question remained unanswered into the 21st century. But after a decade of land war, although disruption continued elsewhere, most Skye crofters were ready to call a truce.

In 1897, still aware of potential unrest in the north-west of the country, not least in those island parishes to which Reverend Donald MacCallum had since been called, the Government established the Congested Districts Board for Scotland. The function of that body was to improve the conditions of over-crowded areas in the Highlands and Islands. Its methods were initially modest. It would distribute seed potatoes, supply stud bulls and assist with the development of such infrastructures as jetties and such home industries as weaving.

Before very long the members of the Congested Districts Board discovered that such amelioratory measures were insufficient in most poor crofting islands and parishes and that they could, if they wished, use their money in other, more transformative ways.

In November 1901 Reverend Hugh Alexander MacPherson died in Pitlochry at the age of 43 years, just twelve months after being inducted as minister to the local church. Hugh MacPherson was still the proprietor of his uncle's Glendale estate, but following his death his wife and his fellow trustees had no interest in keeping the property.

A ready buyer could not be found, and two years later officers of the Congested Districts Board met with crofters in Glendale to discover whether or not they might be interested in leasing the estate. They were. So when the Glendale estate was put up for auction in Edinburgh in December 1903, the Congested Districts Board bought it for £15,000. That sharp decline in the desirability and the market value of Highland estates since the days when MacLeod of MacLeod raised almost £100,000 from the sale of Glenelg was due to the fact that, after 1886, the estates came stocked by crofters who had tenants' rights.

The estate had effectively been nationalised. In 1905, following extensive negotiations at local and national levels, it was delivered into the hands of the community. Glendale would become a self-governing agricultural entity, divorced even from the Crofters' Commission, and administered by an elected committee of five local shareholders. Almost all crofters became small private landholders rather than tenants. The clerk to the first committee was John MacPherson's son Norman.

It took them 50 years to pay off the Government loan, which was finally settled in 1956. They were not easy years. The historian of Glendale estate, George W. MacPherson, recalled that 'My own grandmother was known to have had to resort to walking through the corn to collect individual ripe ears until she had enough to grind into meal between two stones and make thin porridge to feed her family, for there was nothing else.

'To obtain enough money to make the necessary payments was extremely difficult for the people in the early days of the estate. Much of the day-to-day crofting usage was based on a barter system. For example, if you wished to have corn ground into meal, you took your bag of corn and a bag of peat down to the mill. The miller took one-tenth of the corn, and the remainder was dried on the floor of the kiln above a fire of your peats, and ground into meal or flour.

'Swapping of produce between crofters was also widely practised. This did not however bring in cash to pay rates, etc. To overcome this lack of cash it was the custom for the crofter or one or two of his sons or daughters to work away during the summer, or permanently, with a large part of their wages sent home to cover the payments and the costs of the family at home. For example, my father left home at the age of 12 to work on a farm in Perthshire for his keep and £5 per annum, of which £3 was sent home. His brother was also employed as a shepherd and sent most of his salary home. This was a commonplace way of making ends meet. Many also worked at the fishing during the summer months or, in the case of women, in service or fish cleaning. The sale of surplus cattle could not be depended on to cover expenses . . .

'However the use of the larger crofts set out by John Taylor of Eubost, the surveyor employed by the Poor Lands Commission to "lay off" the crofts, eventually alleviated such extremes, and allowed the people to reach a position where they were able to have sufficient corn to arrange to have it ground, in the manner described above, at the watermill at Pollosgan.

'One example of the alterations to the size of the crofts is that of Holmisdale, which was originally four crofts, but was divided by the landlord into 25 crofts, all at the same rent as before. John Taylor reduced the number to 20 crofts. This he considered the maximum viable number, although he felt that the number of crofts could be further reduced with beneficial results. It is worthy of note that the division and layout of the crofts was so well thought of by the crofters that the phrase "A Taylor Home" became established, and lasted for many years as a yardstick of a good croft.'

When John MacPherson died at the age of 87 years in May 1922 at his home in Lower Milovaig, his name still evoked vague memories in the national press. Forty years had passed since MacPherson first made his stand against the excesses of landlords in the Highlands and Islands. A world war had come and gone since he had been twice imprisoned for his beliefs. But some editors and some journalists heard distant bells and recorded in short paragraphs the passing of the Glendale Martyr.

Not one of them, however, pointed out that John MacPherson died on the first (and at the time, the only) community-owned crofting estate in Scotland.

None of the newspapers noted what was common knowledge in Glendale – that John MacPherson had lived to see, over the hill from Lower Milovaig, crofters' sheep and cattle grazing without hindrance on the green turf of Waterstein.

Epilogue

It is easy for a visitor to modern Glendale to note the merest vestiges of a working crofting community, the number of holiday homes and hugely reduced year-round population, and assume that the efforts of the martyrs were either misguided or in vain.

Crofting is a delicate formulation. It was established at a time when almost half of the population of the United Kingdom, and almost all of the population of the Scottish Highlands and Islands, still lived and worked on the land. As we have seen, the premise behind security of tenure for crofters was to give Highlanders a safe toehold in the country of their fathers – to offer them a house, a milking cow, some mutton, root vegetables and grain.

It was never intended to make them rich. Highlanders who sought their fortunes had always done so elsewhere. Nor, obviously enough, could a 19th-century smallholding on the edge of the Atlantic Ocean keep pace financially with the affluence of 20th-century urban Britain.

The compensations for what a City of London trader, or even a Clydeside shipyard welder, would regard as a pitiable wage remained sufficient for many. Even part-time crofting, with the household income supplemented by such other employment as weaving, fishing or delivering the post, is ridiculously hard work.

But it is work that runs in the blood and delivers a familiar, communal satisfaction which those who have known and abandoned it rarely cease to regret. It is work in a glorious environment in the company of good people. Throughout the middle of the 20th century, on the first day of the school holidays railway trains north from Glasgow were packed with children being despatched by their parents back to the family's Highland croft to share at least part of that life among those blue remembered hills.

Slowly, however, such roots were shaken loose. Glendale in the middle of the 20th century was still a busy, hardworking, independent crofting community. Its links to its traditional culture were still strong. Almost everybody born in Glendale before about 1960 was a native Gaelic speaker. In the succeeding decades both crofting and the language of the croft rapidly declined.

That phenomenon was not unique to Glendale. Across the Highlands and Islands, from the glens of Ross and Sutherland to the archipelago of the Outer Hebrides, both the language and the lifestyle slid away as inexorably as sand through an hourglass. To some, the process was simply more painful to observe in a community which had fought for, and apparently won, a more stable future than most of the rest of the region.

When the crofters of Glendale took their estate into democratic communal ownership early in the 20th century, they were treading on virgin soil. They were the first large group of relatively impoverished agricultural tenants in the British Isles to take such a step. There were no precedents to learn from; there was no guidebook to help them on their way.

Although the elected Glendale Estate committee obviously recognised itself as administering an 18,000-acre crofting community, from the outset it stood at a remove from the rest of the crofting world.

Glendale refused, for instance, to register itself with the Crofters Commission. That was understandable. Early in the

20th century the function of the Crofters Commission was largely to liaise between landowners and tenants on such matters as annual rental and grazings apportionment. An independent, self-governing crofting community had no need of outside interference.

Almost all other crofters remained tenants. On those estates which were nationalised and subsequently run by the Board of Agriculture and its successors, such as Kilmuir and Bracadale estates in Skye, the island of Raasay and parts of North Uist, they became tenants of the state. Elsewhere they remained tenants of private landowners, with the securities granted in the 1886 Act.

The crofters of Glendale became owner-occupiers of their individual crofts, each with shares in the estate. They cannot at any time before the Second World War have been expected to realise that the future integrity of crofting estates would depend upon them being tenancies rather than private holdings. In the British property boom of the later 20th century private holdings were inevitably eventually sold on the open market to the highest bidder, even if that bidder lived in Edinburgh or Eastbourne and had no intention of spending more than a few weeks in the year on their new property, let alone working its land.

Secured tenancies, on the other hand, are reassigned by the landowner to another suitable crofting candidate. The Crofters Commission would oversee such assignments, but Glendale was not affiliated to the Crofters Commission.

Glendale's unusual circumstances even left its crofters in an ambiguous position with regard to the government's crofting loan and grant schemes. When the 1955 Crofters (Scotland) Act was passed, it seemed as though owner-occupiers would be excluded from such assistance.

Only a late intervention by the Inverness-shire Conservative MP Malcolm Douglas-Hamilton ensured that Glendale's crofters remained eligible for agricultural and housing subsidies.

The next Hebridean estate to be taken from private hands into community ownership was transferred almost two decades after Glendale. When the town fathers of Stornoway took 70,000 acres of eastern Lewis in trust from Lord Leverhulme in 1923, the extensive crofting land to the north, south, east and west of the burgh, which came as part of the deal, was the least of their concerns. The members of the new Stornoway Trust were more interested in getting their hands on the town's profitable utilities and amenities. They became elected landlords of the crofts almost incidentally. Being Lewismen, they saw little reason to communicate with their forerunner in Skye, let alone copy or learn from Glendale in any way. The crofters of Back and Point in the environs of Stornoway remained tenants, albeit of an accountable local committee which they helped to elect. They preferred things that way. In 1976 another Crofting Reform Act offered them the opportunity to become owner-occupiers. An overwhelming majority of Lewis crofters rejected the opportunity.

After the 1920s there was a 70-year lull in Highland land reform and redistribution. It revived in the spectacular small test cases at Assynt and the island of Eigg in the 1990s. When the Labour Party returned to power in the House of Commons in 1997 and in its newly created Scottish Parliament at Edinburgh in 1999, Highland land reform in particular received government support.

Nationalisation having fallen out of political favour, the urge was once again towards community-owned estates. In the Outer Hebrides the dominoes toppled one by one, until most of that string of populated islands was in local hands.

Everywhere, the pattern followed was that of Stornoway rather than Glendale. Crofters remained tenants of their own community, rather than becoming private smallholders. Glendale, it seemed, was no model for a crofting community to pursue.

That is of practical relevance, but its implications are

historically unfair to Glendale. There is a more just comparison to make. When Lord Leverhulme offered Stornoway and its environs to a local trust in 1923, he also offered the rest of rural, crofting Lewis to a Lewis District Committee on exactly the same terms – free of charge and with no preconditions.

Rural Lewis had far more in common with Glendale than either did with Stornoway. The Lewis District Committee agonised for weeks over the decision. Lewis had also echoed with calls of 'The Land for the People' – not least when such people as John MacPherson of Glendale had visited the island. Now, in 1923, the people were being offered the land.

Unlike the crofters of Glendale, the crofters of rural Lewis refused the offer. Without the assets of Stornoway, Lewis was not a profitable commodity. The rural Leodhasaich and their representatives could not see a way to balance the books. Afraid of personal bankruptcy, they regretfully informed Lord Leverhulme that they had to decline his offer. Rural Lewis was subsequently broken up into several smaller estates and sold on the open market. It remained in private hands until the turn of the 21st century, when a number of communities took on the challenge and bought back their land.

The decision of the Lewis District Committee in 1923 was understandable. It also contrasts vividly with the decision taken by their fellow Hebrideans in rural Glendale a few years earlier. In Glendale, they took the plunge.

The recent history of the Highlands and Islands of Scotland has been neither smooth nor predictable. To the continuing frustration of developers, land reformers and politicians of every party, there has been no panacea for the difficulties of the region's people. What progress has been made is chiefly the result of trial and error. There is no trial greater than assuming custody of ancestral lands and no error more grievous than neglecting them.

The Glendale Martyrs and their contemporaries and their children and their grandchildren passed the trial with red colours flying. They took the first leap into the dark and unforgiving future. Any of their errors are dwarved by that achievement. They helped to win nigh on a century of stability for tens of thousands of Highlanders. Their courage gave the rest of the region time to catch up with their vision. It was no mean feat.

Endnotes

CHAPTER ONE

pp. 2–4:   " 'I have to ask your lordships,' " . . . small adjoining hamlets of
          Upper and Lower Milovaig', Alexander MacKenzie, *The Isle of Skye
          in 1882–1883*
p. 7:   'and on my reaching the . . . rest told him to be quiet', Report to
          Inverness-shire Constabulary, 18 January 1883
pp. 7–9: 'I met at the Fasach side . . . townships of Fasach, Colbost and
          Skinidin', Report to Inverness-shire Constabulary, 18 January 1883
p. 10:   'could not recognise . . . other part of my district', Report to
          Inverness-shire Constabulary, 18 January 1883

CHAPTER TWO

p. 13:   'one valley . . . it scarcely deserves to enjoy,' *The Second Statistical
          Account of Scotland*
p. 14:   'Skie (in the antient language . . . Trotterness North-east)
          resemble two wings', Martin Martin, *Description of the Western
          Islands of Scotland*
p. 15:   'He is just as ourselves . . . subsistence for our families', *Report
          of the Royal Commission of Inquiry into the Condition of Crofters and
          Cottars in the Highlands and Islands*
pp. 15–17: 'The old people affirm . . . much more enterprise than is
          manifested by their descendants', *The Second Statistical Account of
          Scotland*
p. 18:   'Every species of sea-weed . . . the parish makes a hundred tons
          annually', *The First Statistical Account of Scotland*
p. 18:   'At the height of the boom . . . landlords in the shape of rent', *The
          Land Struggle in Skye and Lewis*, Islands Book Trust
p. 19:   'the manufacture of sea-ware . . . and some by stealing', *The
          Second Statistical Account of Scotland*

p. 20:   'Next in dignity to the laird . . . original operation, but not with its primitive stability', Samuel Johnson, *A Journey to the Western Islands of Scotland*

p. 21:   'As the mind must govern . . . will be negligent', Samuel Johnson, *A Journey to the Western Islands of Scotland*

p. 22:   'to every thinking man . . . annually thinned by those who feel the pinching of famine', *The Second Statistical Account of Scotland*

p. 23:   'To give us the land . . . would be no crofters in their way', *Report of the Royal Commission of Inquiry into the Condition of Crofters and Cottars in the Highlands and Islands*

CHAPTER THREE

p. 24:   'comparatively fertile . . . but the bleating of sheep', Joseph Mitchell, *Reminiscences of my Life in the Highlands*

p. 24:   'Where I was born . . . a great stretch of hill pasture', *Report of the Royal Commission of Inquiry into the Condition of Crofters and Cottars in the Highlands and Islands*

pp. 25–27:   'From time immemorial . . . boasted civilisation of the nineteenth century', *Report of the Royal Commission of Inquiry into the Condition of Crofters and Cottars in the Highlands and Islands*

p. 28:   'with medicine and medical advice . . . on my place went away', *Report of the Royal Commission of Inquiry into the Condition of Crofters and Cottars in the Highlands and Islands*

p. 31:   'had spent the best part of . . . with the curry at dinner', Alexander Smith, *A Summer in Skye*

pp. 32–33:   'We told him . . . had overstepped his powers', Calum MacQueen, *St Kilda Heritage: Autobiography of Callum MacCuithinn*

pp. 34–36:   '[MacDonald] had his own code . . . as is perhaps possible', Alexander Smith, *A Summer in Skye*

pp. 36–37:   'We were on . . . of Glendale', *Report of the Royal Commission of Inquiry into the Condition of Crofters and Cottars in the Highlands and Islands*

p. 37:   'When he entered on the direction . . . and he is in port at last', Alexander Smith, *A Summer in Skye*

p. 37:   'Tormore, as a man, was a very good . . . people and properties in the North', Alexander MacKenzie, *The Isle of Skye in 1882–1883*

CHAPTER FOUR

p. 38:   'tenanted by eight crofters . . . if any at all', *Report of the Royal Commission of Inquiry into the Condition of Crofters and Cottars in the Highlands and Islands*

p. 40:   'Poverty was increasing . . . began to fail at first', *Report of the Royal Commission of Inquiry into the Condition of Crofters and Cottars in the Highlands and Islands*

p. 40:   'Without hesitation, the young . . . ended he was totally ruined', Anne Wolrige Gordon, *Dame Flora*

p. 43:   'The men of Glendale are . . . patriotic feelings and ability of their father', Hector Ross MacKenzie, *Yachting and Electioneering in the Hebrides*

p. 49:   'we would humbly pray for . . . similar to other nations', *Report of the Royal Commission of Inquiry into the Condition of Crofters and Cottars in the Highlands and Islands*

p. 50:   'As the land does not get . . . scarce enough for our cattle and sheep', *Report of the Royal Commission of Inquiry into the Condition of Crofters and Cottars in the Highlands and Islands*

p. 51:   'We live in the wildest . . . the [north] shore', *Report of the Royal Commission of Inquiry into the Condition of Crofters and Cottars in the Highlands and Islands*

pp. 51–52: 'ways and means he devised . . . he was not in [rent] arrears', *Report of the Royal Commission of Inquiry into the Condition of Crofters and Cottars in the Highlands and Islands*

pp. 52–53: 'Notice. – Whereas parties . . . Tormore, 4th January, 1882', Alexander MacKenzie, *The Isle of Skye in 1882–1883*

p. 53:   'in the small district of . . . an increase of £2', *Report of the Royal Commission of Inquiry into the Condition of Crofters and Cottars in the Highlands and Islands*

p. 53:   'At one time there were some . . . the shops ceased to exist!', Alexander MacKenzie, *The Isle of Skye in 1882–1883*

p. 54:   'My grandfather Allan Campbell . . . as painfully barbaric as ever', email to the author, 2015

pp. 55–56: 'Emigration is more painful . . . the gorge of the banished!', Alexander Smith, *A Summer in Skye*

CHAPTER FIVE

p. 58:   'I think it would be a mistake . . . improve their lands a little', I.M.M. MacPhail, *The Crofters' War*

pp. 58–59: 'I have built a school-house . . . very sight of a pauper sickens me', Alexander Smith, *A Summer in Skye*

p. 60:   'are poorer than I can tell . . . school for the want of them', *Report of the Royal Commission of Inquiry into the Condition of Crofters and Cottars in the Highlands and Islands*

p. 62:   'We have particular cause . . . of the grazing on Benlee', *Report of the Royal Commission of Inquiry into the Condition of Crofters and Cottars in the Highlands and Islands*

pp. 63–64:   'We have received the . . . a howling crowd of boys',
              Aberdeen Daily Free Press, 10 April 1882

pp. 65–69:   'Arrived at the boundary . . . one of the women seriously
              injured', *Dundee Advertiser*, 20 April 1882

p. 70:   'The prisoners, who had been confined . . . greater part of
              their way to the Braes', Alexander MacKenzie, *The Isle of Skye in
              1882–1883*

p. 73:   'I met two clergymen in the town . . . asked to circulate', *Irish
              World*, 10 June 1882

p. 74:   'discontent in Skye . . . That is my opinion', *Report of the Royal
              Commission of Inquiry into the Condition of Crofters and Cottars in the
              Highlands and Islands*

p. 75:   'I have not the slightest . . . the Irish Land Reform Association in
              Glasgow', *Report of the Royal Commission of Inquiry into the Condition
              of Crofters and Cottars in the Highlands and Islands*

p. 75:   'expression of discontent and rebellion . . . is certainly not
              attributable to Irish agitators', *Report of the Royal Commission of
              Inquiry into the Condition of Crofters and Cottars in the Highlands and
              Islands*

pp. 75–76:   'I know that Tormore . . . he came to this place', *Report
              of the Royal Commission of Inquiry into the Condition of Crofters and
              Cottars in the Highlands and Islands*

p. 77:   ' "I said to Mr Macdonald . . . obliged to carry that with me", '
              *Report of the Royal Commission of Inquiry into the Condition of Crofters
              and Cottars in the Highlands and Islands*

CHAPTER SIX

pp. 78–79:   'are getting indolent . . . I don't see who would take
              them . . .', *Report of the Royal Commission of Inquiry into the Condition
              of Crofters and Cottars in the Highlands and Islands*

p. 79:   'I don't think we made . . . as much rent as they could give', *Report
              of the Royal Commission of Inquiry into the Condition of Crofters and
              Cottars in the Highlands and Islands*

pp. 79–80:   'As I heard the . . . the Prime Minister of the day', email to
              the author, 2015

p. 80:   'I am extremely sorry . . . demands were complied with', *Report
              of the Royal Commission of Inquiry into the Condition of Crofters and
              Cottars in the Highlands and Islands*

pp. 81–83:   'When we heard that Waterstein . . . and I simply walked
              out of it . . .', *Report of the Royal Commission of Inquiry into the
              Condition of Crofters and Cottars in the Highlands and Islands*

pp. 84–85:   'It is as a speaker that John Macpherson . . . feelings of his
              fellow-Highlanders . . ..', Hector Ross MacKenzie, *Yachting and
              Electioneering in the Hebrides*

pp. 85–86: 'three summonses of removal . . . observation of the British Parliament', *Report of the Royal Commission of Inquiry into the Condition of Crofters and Cottars in the Highlands and Islands*

p. 86: 'We are hearing such reports . . . get him to pay for the damage', *Report of the Royal Commission of Inquiry into the Condition of Crofters and Cottars in the Highlands and Islands*

p. 87: 'That we are packed . . . we must needs remain in poverty,' *Report of the Royal Commission of Inquiry into the Condition of Crofters and Cottars in the Highlands and Islands*

p. 87: 'how we are oppressed . . . threaten them with eviction', *Report of the Royal Commission of Inquiry into the Condition of Crofters and Cottars in the Highlands and Islands*

p. 88: 'The awareness of the dire straits . . . his co-leaders to rein in the land leaguers', email to the author, 2015

pp. 88–89: 'was not going with the tenants . . . I must join them again to have peace', Report to Inverness-shire Constabulary, 5 October 1882

pp 92–94: 'As disturbances have recently taken place . . . and aid to the civil authorities . . .', William Ivory to Inverness-shire Police Committee, Skye and Lochalsh Archive Centre

pp. 94–95: 'entitled to have adequate protection . . . they may consider requisite', J.B. Balfour MP to William Ivory, Skye and Lochalsh Archive Centre

pp. 95–96: 'although the County have . . . service for some considerable time', William Grant to Inverness-shire Police Committee, Skye and Lochalsh Archive Centre

p. 96: 'as reported in the . . . as to the grounds of refusal', Hansard, 24 November 1882

CHAPTER SEVEN

p. 99: 'amid the general laughter of the . . . Mr Mackenzie had at heart', Alexander MacKenzie, *The Isle of Skye in 1882–1883*

p. 100: 'Whether his attention . . . a really authentic character', Hansard, 18 June 1881

pp. 100–101: 'If he can explain the circumstances . . . their ordinary bâtons', Hansard, 20 April 1882

p. 102: 'attention has been . . . not in my power', Hansard, 28 April 1882

pp. 104–105: 'he can now state . . . philanthropic interest in the matter', Hansard, 28 November 1882

pp. 105–106: 'Whether Her Majesty's . . . Question put to me just now', Hansard, 30 November 1882

pp. 106–107:   'for what specific services . . . so does constable report
               . . .', letter from J.B. Balfour to William Ivory, Skye and Lochalsh
               Archive Centre

pp. 107–109:   'the following observations . . . unwilling to give a room
               for the one Constable', letter to J B Balfour and William Harcourt,
               Skye and Lochalsh Archive Centre

pp. 110–111:   'There is no other place . . . expect it will be offensive',
               letter from Peter Speirs to Alexander McHardy, Skye and Lochalsh
               Archive Centre

p. 112:   'I was at Station the time . . . getting the warning', Report to
               Inverness-shire Constabulary, 16 January 1883

p. 112:   'When near Hamara . . . report will follow', Report to
               Inverness-shire Constabulary, 16 January 1883

p. 113:   'Word came to our township . . . and we were tired', *Tuath
               is Tighearna (Tenants and landlords: an anthology of Gaelic poetry of
               social and political protest from the Clearances to the Land Agitation
               (1800–1890))*, ed. Donald Meek

p. 114:   'On the last occasion they . . . in his possession', Alexander
               MacKenzie, *The Isle of Skye in 1882–1883*

p. 115:   'The state of matters . . . assumed a state of revolt', letter from
               Alexander McHardy to William Ivory, Skye and Lochalsh Archive
               Centre

CHAPTER EIGHT

p. 119:   'It is the fault of the silly . . . brought us to this', Patrick Jackson,
               Harcourt and Son

p. 119:   'I doubt whether there is anybody . . . them that is singularly
               attractive', Hansard, 11 May 1885

pp. 120–122:   'Inhabitants of Glendale . . . blame but yourselves',
               Glasgow Herald, 6 February 1883

p. 122:   'duine dèanta dìreach . . . could cleave oak', Allan Campbell,
               email to the author, 2015

pp. 122–125:   'repudiated these statements . . . made by the proprietors',
               Alexander MacKenzie, *The Isle of Skye in 1882–1883*

p. 125:   'it was pretty evident . . . by any written statements', *Glasgow
               Herald*, 6 February 1883

p. 126:   'look better, and besides . . . their homes in a man-of-war',
               Alexander MacKenzie, *The Isle of Skye in 1882–1883*

p. 126:   'after bidding farewell . . . Milovaig and Colbost', *Inverness
               Courier*, 13 February 1883

pp. 126–127:   'think there is a chance . . . Commission is promised',
               Glasgow Herald, 13 February 1883

pp. 127–128:   'I wish to ask the Lord Advocate . . . opinion as to its legality', Hansard, 18 February 1883

p. 129:   'The order of the Court . . . trespass would not enter', Alexander MacKenzie, *The Isle of Skye in 1882–1883*

p. 130:   'A few days after . . . He left Waterstein that day . . .', *Edinburgh Evening News*, 12 March 1883

p. 131:   'That interdict . . . the order of the Court', *Edinburgh Evening News*, 14 March 1883

pp 133–134:   'The officials could not . . . during their imprisonment', Alexander MacKenzie, *The Isle of Skye in 1882–1883*

pp. 134–135:   'great surprise and deep sorrow . . . the minds of the people', *Dundee Evening Telegraph*, 7 March 1883

pp. 135–136:   'If his attention . . . and to report thereon", ' Hansard, 19 March 1883

p. 137:   'The landlord party . . . from all parts of Skye', *Dundee Evening Telegraph*, 7 April 1883

p. 137:   'Angus . . . their aid being required', Alexander MacKenzie, *The Isle of Skye in 1882–1883*

p. 138:   'If his attention . . . to observe the law', Hansard, 16 April 1883

pp. 138–139:   'about 1,000 people . . . martyr in the crofter cause', *Glasgow Herald*, 18 May 1883

p. 140:   'When I spoke with the late Neil MacLean . . . suspended above the road – it read "Down with landlords!" ', email to the author, 2015

pp. 141–142:   'I would wish, my Lord and Gentlemen . . . rents for so many years to Government', *Report of the Royal Commission of Inquiry into the Condition of Crofters and Cottars in the Highlands and Islands*

p. 143:   'Many of the allegations . . . of the Highland people', *Report of the Royal Commission of Inquiry into the Condition of Crofters and Cottars in the Highlands and Islands*

CHAPTER NINE

pp. 149–150:   'A system which gave . . . throw the shells away', *Glasgow Herald*, 12 February 1884

pp. 150–151:   'in the forenoon . . . crisis exists in the island', *Aberdeen Evening Express*, 17 October 1884

pp. 152–155:   'With the official responsibility . . . totally unable to sustain their existence', Hansard, 14 November 1884

p. 157:   'an officer on horseback . . . figure on horseback galloping away . . .', Anne Wolrige Gordon, *Dame Flora*

p. 157:   'to confine their agitation . . . objects they had in view', *Glasgow Herald*, 17 November 1884

p. 158:   'To the Crofters . . . as was originally intended', *Glasgow Herald*, 17 November 1884

p. 159:   'he never thought he . . . had no existence whatsoever', *Glasgow Herald*, 17 November 1884
p. 163:   'immediately sought out Sheriff Ivory . . . it would be obeyed', *Aberdeen Evening Express*, 30 January 1885

CHAPTER TEN

pp. 167–168:   'proprietors who have crofting . . . rendered absolutely hopeless', letter from Cameron of Lochiel to William Harcourt
pp. 168–169:   'If the necessities of the persons . . . the crofter's position, though mitigated, would not be removed', letter from John Blair Balfour to William Harcourt
p. 170:   'a fixity or stability of tenure . . . the injury of the community', letter from William Gladstone to William Harcourt
p. 171:   'opposed by Hartington . . . synonymous in his vocabulary', Patrick Jackson, *Harcourt and Son*
p. 173:   'the Crofters Act . . . live on the lands of their native country', *Glasgow Herald*, 18 September 1886
p. 178:   'How are you, John? . . . three cheers for John MacPherson', *Aberdeen Evening Express*, 15 November 1886

Bibliography

Bateman, Meg & Loughran, Anne (eds), *The Glendale Bards*, Edinburgh, 2014

Cameron, A.D., *Go Listen to the Crofters*, Stornoway, 1986

Cameron, Ewen A., *The Life and Times of Fraser Mackintosh, Crofter MP*, Aberdeen, 2000

Cooper, Derek, *Skye*, London, 1970

General Assembly of the Church of Scotland, *The Second Statistical Account of Scotland*, Edinburgh, 1845

Gordon, Anne Wolrige, *Dame Flora*, London, 1974

Grigor, Iain Fraser, *Highland Resistance*, Edinburgh, 2000

Hunter, James, *The Making of the Crofting Community*, Edinburgh, 1976

Islands Book Trust, *The Land Struggle in Skye and Lewis*, Stornoway, 2011

Macdonald, Norman & Maclean, Cailean, *The Great Book of Skye*, Portree, 2014

MacKenzie, Alexander, *The Isle of Skye in 1882–1883*, Inverness, 1883

MacPhail, I.M.M., *The Crofters' War*, Stornoway, 1989

Meek, Donald (ed.), *Tuath is Tighearna* ('Tenants and landlords: an anthology of Gaelic poetry of social and political protest from the Clearances to the Land Agitation (1800–1890)'), Edinburgh, 1995

Newby, Andrew G., *Ireland, Radicalism and the Scottish Highlands, c. 1870–1912*, Edinburgh, 2007

Report of the Royal Commission of Inquiry into the Condition of Crofters and Cottars in the Highlands and Islands, London, 1883

Sinclair, Sir John, *The First Statistical Account of Scotland*, Edinburgh, 1799

Smith, Alexander, *A Summer in Skye*, London, 1865

Index